MISSIONS, MYSTICISM & MAGIC

A Closer Look at the Missionary Organization,
Adventures in Missions

REVISED EDITION

CLARIS VAN KUIKEN

Unless otherwise indicated, all Scripture quotations were taken from the NIV Study Bible, 10th Anniversary Edition, © 1995, The Zondervan Corporation. The Holy Bible, New International Version ® Copyright ©1973, 1978, 1984 by International Bible Society

For more information, you can contact the author at:
clarisj@comcast.net

ISBN-13: 978-1514263846
ISBN-10: 151426384X

DEDICATION

To my precious grandchildren, Krysta, Melanie, Eleanor—and, God willing, future grandchildren: May you continue to grow firm in the faith, always be ready and willing to defend it, and love your Lord and Savior, Jesus Christ, above all else. You will forever have all my love, Grandma.

CONTENTS

AUTHOR'S NOTE

The following open letter was sent to Ingrid Schlueter, former host of Crosstalk, VCY America, a Christian radio program broadcast out of Milwaukee, Wisconsin. My letter, along with the last two chapters, present a very concise, in depth look into the missionary organization, Adventures in Missions (AIM). Embracing concepts found within the New Age movement, the Emergent movement (a new name for a re-packaged form of New Age spirituality), and various Charismatic/Pentecostal streams of thought, *I believe leaders of AIM have created one of the most deceptive forces for "transformational change" in the world today.*

In the name of fulfilling the Great Commission, social justice (socialism), and bringing in God's kingdom on earth, thousands of sincere, young adults who wish to serve Christ on the mission field, are being systematically initiated into the dark world of the occult. They are being nudged towards a different gospel, a different spirit, and counterfeit Christ. From subtle forms of Eastern mysticism seen in the required practice of "listening prayer," to the more blatant occult spiritual beliefs found in alchemy, Magic and sorcery, leaders of AIM have taught and/or supported it all—for the supposed benefit of those eager to find a new, adventurous and fulfilling life in Christ.

I do not probe all facets of the movements mentioned above, name all the countless leaders involved (which would be impossible), or provide details on all those discussed in my letter. However, I believe some of the most crucial characteristics of these movements and how they are being taught by AIM, as well as other missionary organizations, are depicted in their true light. You will see the arrogance of those in authoritative positions become increasingly transparent through their mask of a new, more humble

"Christianity."

The Foreword to this book is Ingrid's answer to my plea for help out of concern for relatives and so many other young adults preparing to go on AIM's mission trip called The World Race. She has put her reputation on the line many times in spite of continuous attacks against her firm stand on the essentials doctrines of the Christian faith and her willingness to expose the way in which false teachings are infiltrating "Christian" churches and schools.

Believe me, this was not an easy or pleasure-filled thing to do—for either of us. Attacks for trying to expose false teachings come from all sides. Sadly, many times they come from the people you least expect—family, friends, "conservative" Christians. But, after carefully examining the facts and prayerfully weighing the consequences of ignoring what is taking place, remaining silent is *not* an option.

Please take the time to read my letter, study it, and discern it. Research the material provided, test everything against Scripture, and if you feel led to do so, share the information with others. While it is not an easy subject to digest, and is definitely *not* something that promises to make you feel good, you will gain needed insight that will help you stand firm in the faith and fight the good fight.

I pray you win the race with a strong determination and fervent love for Jesus Christ!

Claris Van Kuiken

Note: I do not differentiate between the Emerging Church movement and the Emergent movements in this book as some are now doing. In addition, slight changes have been made to the original letter for grammatical purposes and clarity. New information has also been included after the Conclusion.

FOREWORD

Twenty years ago, I was producing the Crosstalk Show and hosting the In Focus program on Channel 30 TV in Milwaukee. I had never heard of contemplative spirituality or the Eastern mysticism that was entering the evangelical church through a number of avenues. A book came across my desk one day called *Trojan Horse: How the New Age Movement Infiltrates the Church*, by Brenda Scott and Samantha Smith. Around the same time, a radio program we had aired on the VCY America Network began airing some bizarre teachings that took people away from the authority of the Scriptures and into the realm of the subjective and mystical. God timed the arrival of that book perfectly as we saw the beginnings of the mainstreaming of contemplative spirituality in Christian radio programming.

We later removed that long time radio program because of the false teachings it was promoting, and through the research we did prior to that, we met not only Brenda Scott and Samantha Smith, but the contributing researcher to their book, Claris Van Kuiken. Claris has been a valuable resource through the years as the emergent church has carried out its onslaught against biblical truth and mainstreamed Eastern mysticism under the guise of Christian spiritual practice. At the same time, the growth of the Manifest Sons of God heresy through the New Apostolic Reformation movement has helped spread mysticism through its own celebrity leaders. The coalescing of these forces has resulted in the diminishing of the belief in Scripture as our way of hearing God's voice and the promoting of individual esoteric experience in hearing the "voice of God." Young people are the targets of this new spirituality that is alien to biblical Christianity.

These movements use familiar jargon, speak of encountering God, prayer and making a difference in the world for Christ, but by the subtlety of these false teachers, they are introducing practices and teachings that go all the way back to the pagan Chaldeans. Satan has no new material. He simply repackages the same old lies for each generation.

I received an open letter this week from Claris Van Kuiken regarding a mission organization that is popular with Christian young people today. Like the Bereans commended in Scripture so many centuries ago, it is more crucial than ever to examine everything being taught by churches and parachurch organizations in the light of Scripture. We cannot afford to trust the spiritual well-being of our young people to leaders who speak passionately and effectively about making a difference in the world for Christ, while at the same time they engage in spiritual practices that are opposed to the teachings of God's Word. I am sharing this letter today in hopes that parents and young adults will examine things closely, not only with this organization but with anything they come across today. Error is rampant, and Scripture-guided vigilance is the watchword. Read the letter!

Ingrid Schlueter

AN OPEN LETTER TO INGRID SCHLUETER, VCY CROSSTALK AMERICA, CONCERNING ADVENTURES IN MISSIONS (AIM)

From: Claris Van Kuiken
Author: *Battle to Destroy Truth: Unveiling a Trail of*
            Deception
Contributing writer and researcher: *Trojan Horse: How*
The New Age Movement Infiltrates the Church by
Samantha Smith and Brenda Scott

December 15, 2010

Dear Ingrid,

A couple of months ago, I received a letter from my niece and her husband who are in their late twenties. In their letter, they shared their excitement about the possibility of going on a mission trip known as The World Race. The mission organization, Adventures in Missions, oversees this "race" which takes them to eleven different countries over a period of eleven months. Because the cost of the mission trip is over fourteen thousand dollars each, they asked for our prayers and financial assistance to help send them off to the mission field. They are scheduled to leave on January 6, 2011.

1

I hadn't heard of AIM before, so curious as to what this organization stood for, I decided to find out more about it. I read numerous posts online by Seth Barnes, AIM's founder, Executive Director, and graduate of Wheaton College; Andrew Shearman, the chairman of the Board of Directors of AIM; Michael Hindes, the Director of the World Race, and Jeff Goins, an employee (staffer) of AIM, as well as other staffers of AIM. I also read books by authors they recommended and those they used favorably to get a point across to their readers. I searched these authors' websites, links to other websites AIM leaders provided, and looked up blogs by former World Race participants to find out what affect this experience had on them. I read the "Parents' Guide" which can be found online for parents of World Racers and Seth Barnes' book, *The Art of Listening Prayer.* His book is *required* reading for all participants of the World Race. Listening prayer is a "spiritual discipline" they *must* practice while on their mission trip.

From everything I've read, it is quite evident that the leaders of AIM have united various Charismatic/Pentecostal streams—The Third Wave, The New Apostolic Reformation, Holy Laughter, the Latter Rain, Manifest Sons of God, Word-Faith, etc., with the New Age/Emergent movement. From the subtlety of contemplative prayer to the blatant occult art of alchemy, these "missionaries" are leading thousands *away* from the Truth into the arms of Eastern/occultic mysticism, or what is known in the occult world as "Esoteric Christianity."

Among the many leaders/authors recommended and positively cited on their posts are: John Wimber, Jack Deere, C. Peter Wagner, Joy Dawson, Cindy Jacobs, Heidi Baker, Brennan Manning, Richard Rohr, M. Scott Peck, Dallas Willard, Henri Nouwen, Richard Foster, Leonard Sweet, Rob Bell, Shane Claiborne, Frank Viola, Mike Yaconelli, Donald Miller, and John Eldredge. Emergent websites such as The Ooze, Emergent Village, Relevant Magazine and Zoecarnate are listed under "Resources" on Jeff Goins' blog. "Wrecked for the Ordinary" is an AIM supported website which will also lead young adults into Emergent thinking.

Both my husband and I have grave concerns not only for our niece and nephew, but for all those planning a mission trip with AIM. Since 1989, from the time Seth Barnes began AIM working from an office in his garage, approximately 80,000 people have participated in both the World Race and AIM's short mission trips. AIM is based in Barnes' hometown of Gainesville, Georgia.

What I found was deeply disturbing, especially in light of the fact Seth Barnes explains: **"Our objective at AIM is to thrust over-protected young people out into the world to formulate their own world view and collide with their destiny.**"[1] This was written in response to a rumor circulating among parents that AIM was a cult because one of their mission teams "went on a one-month media fast." Barnes obviously felt the need to reply and defend their practices of "limited communication" and "silence fasts."

Godly parents are to be honored and cherished. Paul charged Timothy to continue in what he had learned and been convinced of from infancy about the holy Scriptures (2 Timothy 3:14). Yet, the "Parents' Guide" explains the child "must leave the guidance of family" and "belief systems defined by others" *behind* them when they go on the World Race. Why?

The goal of AIM leaders is to have participants "*join in the Great Commission,*" bring "*social justice*" to the oppressed, and "*usher in the kingdom of God on earth.*" They view the World Race as a revolutionary movement of radicals out to change the world. Similar to the Charismatic concept of Joel's Army, they're looking to enlist an "army" of youth to bring the world back to the perfect state of the Garden of Eden.

4 / *Missions, Mysticism & Magic*

Like Brian McLaren, Rick Warren and other Emergent leaders who say we need to "cast a vision" and see "God's preferable future," leaders of AIM refer to the Great Commission found in Matthew 28:18-19 to describe our responsibility to bring "heaven to earth." However, I have yet to see them refer to Mark 8:15-16. After telling the disciples to go out and preach the gospel to all nations, Jesus adds: "Whoever believes and is baptized will be saved, *but whoever does not believe will be condemned*" (emphasis added). Is their vision wishful thinking? Or, is it purposeful disregard of Scripture?

In a testimony written by World Racer, Chelsea DiPaolo, she admitted having "panic at launch." But, she continued, "Michael Hindes, the director of the World Race, told us that *our willingness to change would be the lynchpin to ushering the Kingdom in during our time.*"[2]

For these young people to be told *they* can bring in the kingdom of God and that they *must* change in order to do so is alarming. The crucial question is, what must they change and how will they change it?

There is also a "demand" placed upon World Racers to "mature" in the faith. Part of the maturing process is seeking the ability to "wield his [Jesus'-cvk] delegated authority and power." This includes raising people from the dead and casting out demons—even from Christians. Seth Barnes told their anxious team in Peru "to sit tight, that they would get 'to do the stuff.'"[3]

In describing "the change process," Barnes speaks of "Mission trips as "spiritual formation."[4] Unfortunately, he uses humanistic, transpersonal psychologist, Abraham Maslow, to discuss spiritual growth.[5] Providing a picture of Maslow's famous pyramid, the Hierarchy of Needs, Barnes insists to his readers that they need "mentors," "coaches" and "discipleship" in order to reach "the highest level – self-actualization" (similar to the concept of Self-realization in Hinduism).

Why would Barnes use Maslow, whose works have been so influential in the New Age movement, to talk about spiritual growth? Appealing to the so-called wisdom of the mystics, Barnes and other AIM leaders/staffers believe the World Race is an opportunity to go on a "pilgrimage," a "journey of self-discovery," in order to find one's "true self." Andrew Shearman, also founder of the G42 (the 42nd Generation) Leadership Academy in Spain, tells World Racers it is their destiny to "become God with skin on."[6]

Before he died, Maslow refuted his theories that were based on the idea that humans were inherently good. Today, however, transpersonal psychologists "serve as intermediaries in the ongoing East/West dialogue and translate the mystical language of Eastern spirituality into psychological terms that make sense to Western students. Similarly, they help Eastern teachers communicate their teachings to Westerners with greater effectiveness."[7]

Tragically, AIM leaders have embraced what Maslow later refuted.

When Western society, capitalism, the Western concept of God, and the "American" church are continually being denounced, and practicing various forms of Eastern/occultic meditation is said to be a necessary "spiritual discipline," there is good reason to believe the gospel being promulgated is a "different gospel." Such is the case with AIM.

There are many positive aspects of AIM—aiding the sick, helping the poor and needy, bringing awareness to the travesty of human trafficking, AIDS, and doing other good works. But,couched in the language of humility and justice, cloaked in Christian terminology, disguised in the euphoria of experience and doing good works, lies a gospel diametrically opposed to the historic, essential tenants of the Christian faith: the unique authority of Scripture, the unique divinity of Jesus Christ, the substitutionary atonement, and the final separation between believers and unbelievers.

Barnes "realized how the The World Race is a pioneer church-planting and discipleship program" (see "John Eldredge on community living").[8] Instead of reaching thousands with the saving knowledge of the gospel of Jesus Christ, the World Race will be advancing the work of those dedicated to destroying the "old, old story." The gospel will be replaced with the "New Story" found in the "ancient wisdom" of mediums and mystics.

There is much that could be said about this organization. In fact, a whole book could be dedicated to it. But I wanted to provide you with just a few examples of why I see AIM to be so detrimental to the faith and some of the documentation to support my conclusions. If you feel led by God to share it with others, please, by all means, do so.

THE ART OF LISTENING PRAYER

One of the "core values" of AIM is that of "Listening Prayer." As I mentioned earlier, all participants in the World Race are *required* to read Seth Barnes' book, *The Art of Listening Prayer* (2005). Not only are they to read it, they *must* practice this "spiritual discipline" during their eleven month long "adventure." In his book, Barnes informs participants of the World Race that in silence and solitude, they'll be able to recognize the "still, small voice of God."[9] It's possible, Barnes claims, to hear "God's" voice audibly, as well as through impressions, dreams and visions, which he believes are all necessary in order to *really* know God and have a relationship with Him. He also encourages his readers to keep a journal and write down what they think God might be saying to them.

On one hand, before practicing this discipline, Barnes tells his readers that they need to "ask for protection in Jesus' name from deception."[10] On the other hand, he complains: "We're so saturated with doctrine that has little or no basis in our experience that we look and act like hypocrites."[11] There is a whole lot more behind his reason for saying this. Barnes is skeptical of being able to fully know the meaning of *any* passage of the Bible, except for "the Ten Commandments" and "a number of precepts." That, says Barnes, "leaves a lot that is open to interpretation."[12]

Tragically, Barnes' assumption leaves the door wide open for the possibility of a different gospel, a different spirit and a different Christ to "emerge" (2 Corinthians 11:4). Thwarting off accusations against what he is teaching throughout his numerous blog posts, Barnes writes: "When Christians say something 'is not biblical,' they often are treating the Bible as though it were not open to interpretation."[13] When young people read this, how many will question Barnes or other AIM leaders, who, in their trusting eyes, are wonderful, Christian leaders cleansing the world of evil?

Placing sound doctrine on a much lower level of importance than the hallowed experience of hearing God's voice and being able to perform all the miracles Jesus did, Barnes quips: "Sometimes orthodoxy is over-rated. Faith is trust in a person, not espousing a set of beliefs."[14]

I have to differ with Barnes. Isn't it both? Didn't Jesus ask Peter: "Who do you say that I am?" (read Luke 9:18-23). How do you know the person without knowledge of God's revelation of that person? Wouldn't this knowledge be a set of beliefs about that person? All the warnings Jesus and the apostles gave us concerning false Christs and false prophets of righteousness are tossed aside by this statement and similar ones found sprinkled throughout his posts.

CHARISMATIC MADNESS

I believe *The Art of Listening Prayer* is an initiation into Eastern/occultic mysticism. The works he recommends for reading at the end of his book will carry his readers deeper into the "spiritual discipline" of contemplative prayer, the prophetic, the Third Wave (signs and wonders movement), and much more. They are:

Hearing God, Dallas Willard
Hearing God, Peter Lord
Intercession, Joy Dawson
Communion with God, Mark Virkler
When God Speaks, Henry & Richard Blackaby
Surprised by the Power of the Spirit, Jack Deere
Surprised by the Voice of God, Jack Deere
Listening Prayer, Leanne Payne
The Voice of God, Cindy Jacobs
The Hour that Changes the World, Dick Eastman
Rees Howells, Intercessor, Norman Grubbs

Some of the authors listed are also promoted by Youth With A Mission, another organization my niece has gone on mission trips with. Steven Mitchell, of Power to Stand Ministries, wrote an open letter dated February 2002, to Calvary Chapel Pastors of America Concerning YWAM.[15] He warns them about the "dangerous teachings" being held by YWAM adherents and the "potential spiritual health hazard awaiting many of our young people" if they are sent to YWAM's Discipleship Training Schools. Mitchell also decries Joy Dawson's support of "faith healer" Benny Hinn, who claims we are all little Messiahs, and the unbiblical spiritual warfare practices being used by false prophetess Cindy Jacobs,

Jack Deere, "chief apostle" of The New Apostolic Reformation, C. Peter Wagner, and others.

What did I learn from reading many of these works and researching the authors' websites? Those who hold onto the sufficiency of Scripture are seen as less mature in the faith and scolded as "Bible deists." The only way to *really* know God is by hearing God's voice. Receiving the "anointing" is much more important than holding on to sound doctrine. The "anointing" means you've been given the ability to perform all the miracles Jesus did, including raising the dead and casting out demons. You will be able to talk with "the Lord" on a regular basis and receive new revelations and prophesies from him (making you *feel* all warm and fuzzy inside). It doesn't matter if your prediction doesn't occur; you're not a false prophet. You'll begin to *experience* all sorts of "manifestations" of the Holy Spirit that will affirm your "anointing." You can bring down strongholds of demons by using spiritual warfare techniques such as prayer-walking, spiritual mapping, binding territorial spirits, spreading oil, drawing crosses, driving stakes around property and whatever other techniques might "work." This will enable Christians to crush the enemy and bring in the kingdom of God in triumph.

In Seth Barnes post, "Heidi Baker expects miracles – so should you," he encourages his readers to learn from John Wimber's experience of seeing God release his healing power—something "God wants all of his children to learn."[16] Through the works of Wimber and Jack Deere, who served with Wimber at Vineyard Christian Fellowship Church in Anaheim, CA, young adults will be introduced to "The Toronto Blessing" and "Holy Laughter." Supposedly, thanks to Rodney Howard-Browne, the Holy Laughter man from South Africa, we can "catch" the Holy Spirit and laugh mindlessly for hours on end. I hate to think what these young people are being introduced to!

Wimber and Browne teach you what "real" manifestations of the "Holy Spirit" are. You may *feel* something like a lightening bolt passing through you, *experience* spasmodic jerking, uncontrollable shaking, sliding out of your seat to the floor in side-splitting laughter, and being stuck to the floor like glue. You might even find yourself being thrown across a room (don't worry, its gotta be the Holy Spirit). You can have a whole lot of fun if you just open up your mind to receive whatever "the Spirit" gives you. You may *experience* the "high" of being drunk while preaching a sermon, "pogoing"(uncontrollable, continuous jumping up and down), howling like wolves, oinking like pigs, barking like dogs, speaking in tongues (interpreter isn't needed), and see miracles like "holy rain" come down on "anointed men." Holy Rain is rain water inexplicably appearing on you—as Seth Barnes positively points out about what happened to Todd Bentley at the "Lakeland Revival."[17]

Though Barnes admits there were excesses by Bentley (like kicking, hitting, and jumping on a person's back to heal them perhaps?), he still believes the revival was "fruitful." Never-mind the fact Bentley boasted of having his own spirit guide in the form of an "angel" called Emma. According to Bentley, she also helped William Branham with his healing ministry. Branham declared he was Elijah, the Trinity to be a pagan doctrine, that Jesus was not deity or Eternal, and the zodiac was just as valid as the Word of God.[18] I don't think Bentley's "Emma" was even close to being an angel!

Guy Chevreau admits in his book, *The Toronto Blessing: An Experience of Renewal and Revival: Catch the Fire*, that you won't find "pogoing" in Scripture at all. He writes: "To my knowledge, there is no Biblical parallel, or basis for such a physical manifestation of the Spirit's power and presence on a person."[19] That doesn't make a difference to Chevreau. It seems his only criteria for knowing if these manifestations are from God is whether or not they make "the person love Jesus more." But, which Jesus will they be showing their devotion to? If these manifestations were signs of being mature in the faith, wouldn't we see something similar to this in Scripture? In total contrast to the teachings of these blind, charismatic leaders, Paul told Titus: "You must teach what is in accord with sound doctrine. Teach the older men to be temperate, worthy of respect, self-controlled, and sound in faith, in love and in endurance" (Titus 2:1-2).

Several years ago, I was invited to speak in Illinois at a Concerned Women for America meeting. Towards the end of my talk, I showed this group of discerning women excerpts of a video on the Toronto Blessing and the revival at Brownsville in Pensacola, Florida. Even those from Charismatic backgrounds were stunned at what they saw. Thankfully, they knew instantly the Holy Spirit had nothing to do with the kind of chaos they had just witnessed.

Of all the works Barnes recommends, I found Mark Virkler's book, *Communion with God*, most disconcerting. Guiding his readers on how to hear "God's" voice, he advises: "Of paramount importance is learning to break free from the prison of rationalism in which Western culture is locked and relearning how to have spiritual experiences..."[20] Sounding like a New Age medium, Virkler discusses left-brain, right-brain thinking and the need to rely more upon the right hemisphere's intuitive and visionary functions. This way, he believes we can make direct spiritual contact with God and get into His divine "flow," and into "true spiritual Christianity."[21] On Sid Roth's program, "It's Supernatural," Virkler teaches Roth and his viewers how to hear God's voice and journal it down.[22]

Watching Virkler is no different than watching a medium teach you how to channel a spirit guide and instruct you in the occult art of automatic handwriting. Sticking "God's" name on this activity doesn't make it any less occultic; it just makes it more deceptive. God condemns occult beliefs and practices for a reason (e.g. Deuteronomy 18:10-22; Leviticus 20:6).

I found an example of the "benefits" of journaling on Virkler's Communion with God Ministries website. Michael Holden, a "student" of Virkler, tells the "Lord" he wants "more anointing" and asks him how to get it. Appealing to Holden's ego, "God" answers:

> If you want the anointing to the level in which I functioned, then you must be prepared to drink the same cup and listen to the Father as I did...There is the potential in every Christian to raise the dead...
>
> My power – energy in the spiritual realm – is needed to accomplish spiritual things...
>
> Always keep yourself open to learning more. My revelation gifts are part of my grace. Never ever think or believe you have arrived. Always there is more. Truth – seek truth. Never be content to rest in your current understanding. Press on, but be sure that it is toward Me, always toward Me, rather than the "thing." My blessing will be yours, Michael. I love you.

After telling Michael never to be satisfied with what he already knows to be truth, the "Lord" entices: "When you have become a cleansed vessel there is no limit to the power that can be released. Only believe that all things are possible, for it is My power at work and has nothing of dependence on you."[23]

If you compare the instructions Seth Barnes and Mark Virkler provide on journaling God's voice, to the instructions Barbara Marx Hubbard gives on journaling in her book, *Emergence*, you'll find there is basically no difference whatsoever.[24]

I don't believe it's a coincidence that this New Age medium, who claims to channel Christ, declares "Christ" told her we can have all the powers Jesus had.[25] I may not agree with Dave Hunt on everything, but he has good reason for saying Virkler's book, *"Dialogue With God,* seduces Christians into contact with demons masquerading as 'God' and 'Christ.'"[26]

Like well-known occultists and contemplative leaders who are influencing millions today, Barnes and Virkler use the Lord's words, "Be still and know that I am God," found in Psalm 46:10, for support of their teachings. Yet, this text has absolutely nothing to do with learning a "new" way to have a two-way conversation with God. In this verse, God's voice breaks through to address His people telling them not to be alarmed and, to their comfort, know that He is God and will be exalted. They weren't using a technique to hear Him.

God informs us that His thoughts are *not* our thoughts and His ways are *not* our ways; they are higher than ours (Isaiah 55:8-9). These presumptuous teachers, however, assure us we can know them by hearing His voice in our own imaginations. You would think that reading Ezekiel 13 and similar passages in Scripture condemning "those who prophecy out of their own imaginations," would stop them in their tracks. But, it seems Barnes and Virkler believe they can verify revelations or experiences are from God by using what Barnes terms "debriefing." If, after sharing a revelation or experience with others, at least two or three people (your spiritual advisors according to Virkler), also believe what was given came from God, you have confirmation that it was, most likely, from God. The problem is, if all of them are involved in practices God forbids, how can anything heard or experienced be from God? Sadly, by placing experience *over* doctrine, Barnes and Virkler have lost their way to Truth.

In *The Art of Listening Prayer*, Barnes recalls one

situation in which a member of a ministry team told his leader about a disturbing, "clear impression" he received from the Lord. Supposedly, "the Lord" told him that Paul Miller and his wife were going to die in two months. What happened? Miller put his things in order and in two months there was a car accident that killed both he and his wife.[27] Did that impression come from the Lord?

Experience and feelings have trumped sound doctrine and overridden sound judgment. Inevitably, the unique divinity of Jesus Christ will be denied and all paths to God will be embraced. For that reason, it's critical to take a closer look at the objective of AIM and the World Race.

THE WORLD RACE—A JOURNEY OF SELF-DISCOVERY?

Seth Barnes believes the World Race to be a "commitment to a transformational discovery process" that "taps an ancient human compulsion to take a spiritual pilgrimage." It is a "rite of passage – an initiation into adult life" which Barnes says "is a forgotten practice in the West."[28]

In his message, "Adventures in Missions 'World Race' for January 2011," Goins acknowledges: "According to Seth Barnes, executive director of AIM, the program is an 'initiation process' that takes participants on an 'epic pilgrimage.'"[29]

Sounding much closer to typical, misguided New Age gurus than God-fearing missionaries, Barnes and Jeff Goins see the World Race as a journey of *self-discovery* and an opportunity for *spiritual formation.* Leaving home (abandonment), they say, is essential in order to find one's "true identity," the "true self." The process of abandoning (leaving home) is critical to rid the World Racer of the "false self," which Barnes sees as "the ego."[30]

It wasn't hard to figure out where their ideas came from. Barnes, Goins, and others involved with AIM, find Franciscan mystic, Richard Rohr, fascinating. In his post, "Rohr on becoming a spiritual warrior," Barnes entices World Racers with this mystic's blasphemous gospel and different Christ saying, "Richard Rohr is so profound – probably the wisest man I've met."[31]

For those reading this who don't know him, Rohr is founder of the Center for Action and Contemplation in Albuquerque, New Mexico, and author of several books, including *Quest for the Grail* and *Enneagram 11: Advancing Spiritual Discernment*. The Enneagram is often praised as a psychological tool used for the purpose of self-discovery, but is said to have ties to a mixture of various ancient wisdom (occult) traditions. Sufi mysticism, alchemy, astrology, and Madonna's favorite, the Cabala (or Kabbalah), the books of Jewish mysticism, all seem to have played a role in the development of the Enneagram. Rohr describes this system, consisting of nine personality types, as "an interesting way to self-knowledge," a tool for "spiritual conversion" and "transformation of consciousness."[32]

Rohr preaches the "cosmic Christ" theology Matthew Fox espouses. Fox, a controversial Dominican priest who was silenced temporarily by the Vatican in 1988, is author of *The Coming of the Cosmic Christ*. In his book, Fox says we have been too preoccupied with the historical Jesus, and that we have "to move from a 'personal Savior' Christianity—which is what an anthropocentric and anti-mystical Christianity gives us—to a 'cosmic Christ' Christianity..."[33] He explains: "We are all Cosmic Christs, other Christs."[34] The "Cosmic Christ...lives and breathes in Jesus and in *all* God's children, in all the prophets of religion everywhere, in all creatures on the universe."[35] For an unrepentant Fox, the cosmic Christ is "...the 'Buddha Nature' that's in all of us, if you're a Buddhist. It's the divine light that's in all of us."[36]

Fox's staff has included Starhawk, a practicing witch; Juisah Teish, a Voudon Priestess; Buck Ghost Horse, a Native American Shaman (witchdoctor); an Episcopal priest who became a Zen Buddhist; and a Yoga instructor. Worshiping the earth as God's body, a living breathing organism known as the Goddess Gaia, Fox has revived paganism in all its God-defying glory.

You can see Rohr's assortment of books, DVD's, CD's and MP3's at the Center's website. Some of the titles available are Cosmic Christ, Christ, Cosmology and Consciousness, Jesus and Buddha: Paths to Awakening, Following the Mystics, Enneagram Intensive: Relationship to Self, God & Others, and Emerging Church: Christians Creating a New World Together. The Wisdom School taught by Richard Rohr states the goal is "not only to deepen our personal spiritual lives, but *to raise human consciousness, leading to the ultimate transformation of society.*"[37]

In his post, "Richard Rohr: A Conversation," Barnes writes that he "met Richard Rohr at a retreat center in Atlanta for an extended conversation in 2006." He "read a few of Rohr's books and found his insights profound." After reading Rohr's book, *Adam's Return*, they discussed initiation rites for men. Barnes then told Rohr about "the World Race and asked him for advice about how to design it to *initiate* young people."[38]

Barnes continued his conversation with Rohr, turning to the subject of "spiritual growth." He revealed: "Another of Rohr's books, *Everything Belongs,* has been a huge influence in my thinking about how we grow." Barnes then wrote about the importance of making "quiet time," debriefing, discipleship, and getting rid of the "material eye." Towards the end of his brief message, Barnes tells his readers he asked Rohr to pray for him and that the "great saint's anointing" gave him a "wonderful blessing." Rohr had led him to the bookstore where Barnes said he showed him "a bunch of stuff he'd written" and "CD's of talks" he'd given. Barnes had "bought so much of it," he was still going through it. "We need to search the Scriptures as an aid to growth and we need to interact with men like Rohr whom God has blessed with spiritual insight,"[39] he concluded.

From Rohr's "wonderful book, *Everything Belongs*," Barnes gleans his New Age/Emergent gospel which, in total contradiction to Scripture, teaches we need to get rid of our "false self," find our "true self," and bring in God's kingdom on earth. "Your true self is like Jesus' vision of the kingdom – a pearl of great price waiting to be discovered," as Barnes so convincingly puts it. "*Initiation* merely tries to direct, facilitate, and speed up the process of REDISCOVERING our true self."[40]

In occult literature, "initiation" involves the beginning process of delving deeply into the "mysteries of God." More precisely, it's an initiation into mysticism. "Discipleship" refers to the ongoing process by which the "disciple" is taught the ways of the mystic—the spiritual practice of finding "the God within."

In Scripture, the human, true self is seen as corrupted by the fall in the Garden and sin is imputed to all through Adam (Romans 5:17). However, the "true self," according to Barnes, is the internal, "spirit man" within each person. In New Age/Emergent thought this is a reference to the "Divine Self" or the "god within." The goal is to *emerge* from one's lower self to one's Higher Self. This is *not* to be confused with the process of sanctification in which Christians strive to be like Jesus until His return and sin is forever vanquished.

Various forms of Eastern/occultic meditation are pivotal

to the formation of the Higher, Divine Self. Contemplative or centering prayer, deep-breathing exercises until one reaches an altered state of consciousness, chanting mantras, yoga, visualization, out-of-body experience/astral projection, are a necessary part to becoming a "Christ" like Jesus did. Through these practices and our own sacrifices and suffering (the way of the cross), we, supposedly, can follow Jesus into our own divinity (godhood) and usher in the kingdom of God on earth—a new age of peace and enlightenment.

Our problem isn't original sin (sin inherited to us through Adam-Romans 5:12), it's just that humans forgot who we truly are. Using Emergent author, John Eldredge, Barnes adds to the confusion: "We are not what we were meant to be, and we know it." He asserts: "The fact that we don't see our own glory is part of the tragedy of the Fall; a sort of spiritual amnesia has taken all of us." Quoting Chesterton, Barnes concludes: "Every man has forgotten who he is...We are all under the same mental calamity; we have all forgotten our names. We have all forgotten what we really are."[41]

In *Everything Belongs,* which means everything is part of God, therefore, everything will be saved, Rohr writes:

> I personally do not believe that Jesus came to found a separate religion as much as he came to present a universal message of vulnerability and foundational unity that is necessary for all religions, the human soul, and history itself to survive. Thus Christians can rightly call him "the Savior of the World..."

> The Cosmic Christ is no threat to anything but separateness, illusion, domination, and any imperial ego. In that sense, Jesus, the Christ, is the ultimate threat, but first of all to Christians themselves. Only then will they have any universal and salvific message for the rest of the earth.[42]

Barnes says he and his wife will be more than happy to help those struggling with their false self to find their true identity:

> If you're still stuck in an old identity that isn't the real you, do yourself a favor and trust yourself to someone who loves you enough to help you find your true self in all the sparkling glory that God intended when he first thought you up.[43]

As in other articles I've read, parents are seen as the likely problem because they have largely been responsible for defining the way their child perceives themselves.

Underneath the "helpful" suggestions Seth Barnes may give, comes something spiritually dark that will undermine parents who have taught their children the wonderful truths of Scripture. After providing a few good examples of people who changed their lives, Barnes writes: "They all decided to trust people who spoke life and truth about who they really are and who God intended them to be." He goes on to quote them as saying: "'Those people didn't know the real me. They didn't believe in my core, and they weren't trustworthy. I'm going to exchange what they said about who I am with what God says.'" Once again, Barnes' assessment undermines parents, whether he means to do so or not: "Instead of living according to some default setting from childhood, they chose to believe truth and trust the re-formation of their identity to trustworthy people who could see their real, core self,"[44] writes Barnes. Guess who some of those trustworthy people are.

SOCIAL JUSTICE REVOLUTIONARIES

Another aspect of AIM is the emphasis on "social justice," a polite, innocuous name for *socialism*. Interestingly, Richard Rohr is a contributing writer for the very progressive magazine, *Sojourners,* the editor of which is Jim Wallis, spiritual advisor to President Obama and self-avowed Marxist.

Decrying the Western American church, materialism, and "American's shallow spiritual lives" is a theme found throughout the many writings of AIM's leaders and staffers. It's pointed out by Jeff Goins and in the "Parents' Guide," that World Racers are "disenchanted with the American church" and the "luxurious, yet unhappy Western world.[45] Barnes complains that he was "raised in our cynical American culture" and that "most American Christians would not have a clue what to do with the enemy."[46]

The overall tone throughout Barnes' posts suggests that Western culture has been inadequate, too rationalistic, oppressive and evil. There is a continuous call for social justice, the redistribution of wealth, and a battle against the evils of oppression, materialism and capitalism. This sounds strikingly similar to the transformational change President Obama and Jim Wallis have in mind for the United States. Perhaps that's because bringing "justice" to the world and creating utopia here on earth is part of the *new* gospel being taught to unsuspecting young Christians at AIM training camps.

In his post, "Vote for Jesus this presidential election," Seth Barnes reveals, once again, where his mind is. He admits he became "a fan" of Emergent author, Shane Claiborne, ever since reading his book, *Irresistible Revolution,* and then provides a review of Shane's book, *Jesus for President.*[47] Claiborne is a social activist, mystic, and New Monastic leader.

Like a revolutionary Claiborne would love, Barnes posted a "vision" that came from the group known as 24-7 Prayer. "The vision is an army of young people" who "are free from materialism." They are an army of "Revolutionaries" willing to lay down their life "for the cause." An army that is

disciplined, who "beat their bodies into submission."
Whatever it takes, this army of young people are the warriors
who will bring down the strongholds of demons. "Their
prayers summon the hounds of heaven and invoke the ancient
dream of Eden."[48]

I never heard of the phrase "hounds of heaven," but I have
certainly heard the phrase "hounds of hell." *Summoning* the
hounds of heaven and *invoking* the dream of Eden? Where in
Scripture do we see believers summoning and invoking
anything? You won't find it in Scripture, but you will find it in
books of sorcery, witchcraft, and other occult works.

Similar to the vision of the 24-7 Prayer group, Barnes
wants to build an army of youth to form "the 42nd generation"
which he and Andrew Shearman hope will usher in the
kingdom of God on earth, transforming the world back into the
Garden of Eden before the fall. "God is interested in speaking
to us and partnering with us to bring his kingdom to earth,"
Barnes wrote in "How God spoke this morning."[49]

THE 42nd GENERATION—SEPARATING JESUS FROM CHRIST

Who is the 42nd generation? In Matthew 1:17, if you add
up the number of generations given between Abraham and
Christ, you come up with 42. But, when Shearman actually
counted them separately, there were only 41. Well, it dawned
on Andrew Shearman as he read Matthew 1, that the 42nd
generation had to be "that Jesus the Christ was the 42nd
generation." It's the generation that comes to faith, receives its
inheritance from God and gets "the Promised Land."

Separating Jesus from Christ, Seth Barnes asks his
readers:

The 42nd generation is the one that goes from Jesus, Son of Man, to Jesus Son of God, to the Christ. I believe that generation is alive on the earth today. Are you a part of it?[50]

Once again, separating Jesus from Christ, Barnes insists, "The 42nd generation is *between Jesus and Christ.*"[51] How can this generation of youth be *between* Jesus and Christ? Does he mean they need to strive to be more like Jesus and help to make a difference in the world? Or, is it much deeper than that? In another post, Barnes adds:

> The condition of the world does not mean that Christ cannot conquer it. *We can cross the Jordan if we have Christ formed in us.* Where are the men and women who say we are here to change the world and we will enlarge our world? The valley of dry bones in Ezekiel turned into a vast army...
>
> At 30 years of age, suddenly his [Jesus'-cvk] life changed. *He declared, "I am the Christ." The Bible says as a man thinks in his heart, so he is.* He who rules his own spirit is stronger than he who takes a city. Out of the abundance of the heart, the mouth speaks. We need a pure heart.[52]

Why does Barnes separate Jesus from Christ in the above quote? After Jesus' declaration, how can he add, "the Bible says as a man thinks in his heart, so he is?" What has he just done? Hasn't he just declared, in so many words, that as Jesus became Christ so must we? Either Barnes says things in a very weird way, is very mixed up, or he knows exactly what he's saying and is presenting a different gospel to his readers.

In order for World Racers to "grow up" they need to put on their "anointing," become warriors in battle, and *Come to faith in the Christ in them.*"[53] "Jesus was the man part of God and Christ is the God-part," writes Barnes. "Yes they are one and the same, but they are also different. The 42nd generation that this text [Matthew 1:16] is talking about not only was Christ himself, but also is us, the body of Christ. And to that extent, the 42nd generation will come about when Christ is formed in us as the body of Christ."[54]

In an interview with AIM's chairman, Andrew Shearman, Barnes asks what is meant to have Christ formed in you. "Jesus, Savior, Christ, something else – what does that mean?" quizzes Barnes.[55]

Shearman's answer is confusing, perplexing, contradictory and misleading. Keep in mind the influence mystics have had on AIM's leaders as you read his answer. Then you may want to sort it out by testing his answer against Scripture. This interview is part four of a five-part series about the 42nd generation. It takes watching all five interviews with Shearman to get a clearer picture of what he believes. This is his reply:

> Christ, Lord, Messiah, Anointed One, Jesus – it gives you himself for nothing. Christ is formed in you. It becomes a process. The process is engaged in through choice. The choice is to die or be killed. It's a massive process. And, of course, Paul...says to the people he's writing to, I labor, I strive, I'm like a pregnant woman trying to give birth to you so that Christ will be formed in you..."[56]

Towards the end of the interview, Shearman insists that he doesn't want to get into heresy. Wanting to make that perfectly clear, he adds: "Jesus and Christ are not two different people...Jesus was God, is God, and always will be God."[57] But, has he stayed away from heresy?

There is much more to the story. "He [Jesus], Shearman

continues, "died and became a man. But that's what has to happen. Our humanity has to be dressed with divinity. *We can and should be, God with skin on. That's what we're really destined to be.*"[58] In all my life, I have never heard such a statement. I suppose you could take his declaration to mean people should see Christ through our actions and the love we show to others. But, knowing all of whom AIM's leaders are entranced with, I don't believe this is the case.

Let me give you a summary of the other four, rather short interviews. What sounds like the Catholic notion that works are necessary for salvation, Shearman talks about people being saved, performing miracles, and more, but, they're still disinherited. He doesn't provide much of an answer except, possibly, that it was the lack of forming Christ in them. He details his belief that in order to receive our "inheritance" we must choose to die (to self) or be killed (crushed by the Rock who is Christ).[59] We must "incarnate" the Word like Jesus did. "Jesus you get for nothing," says Shearman, but "Christ will cost you everything." We get "God's DNA" from Jesus, but it has to be formed "in order to get our inheritance."[60] It dawned on him: "I got Jesus my savior. Jesus means savior. The world needs a savior. The world has never been without a savior. You get him [Jesus-cvk], for nothing; Christ, the 42nd generation, to get the inheritance, has to be formed in us."[61] "God is waiting for a generation that will make the 42nd move...which is the world and all that is therein."[62]

I find Shearman's statement about heresy rather curious since Seth Barnes, Jeff Goins, and other AIM advocates have no problem leading their readers to mystic Richard Rohr who proclaims a different "cosmic christ." It is precisely the mystics they have turned to for their answers. Goins makes this perfectly clear: "The mystics understood something that we often forget—the only way to save the world is to leave it."[63] Does God ask us to save the whole world, or preach the gospel to all nations?

French, Jesuit priest and mystic, Pierre Teilhard de Chardin, whose works have deeply influenced New Age thought, also promoted the concept of a cosmic Christ as the consciousness found within all creation. He believed both humans and the world to be in an upward, evolutionary process, and as "co-creators" with God, humans had the responsibility to bring the world to the Omega Point, or what Teilhard termed, "Christification." The world becomes, in a sense, the body of Christ.[64]

Occultists like Theosophist and medium, Alice Bailey, also use Colossians 1:27 where it reads "which is Christ in you, the hope of all glory," or Galatians 4:19 where it states, "until Christ is formed in you," to justify their belief that we can become Christ like Jesus did. That's also why they believe we can have all the powers Jesus had. According to Sid Roth and Mark Virkler, having these powers is "normal." The ones who don't possess these powers are the abnormal ones—immature Christians who have yet to see the light as to what Christianity is really about. Since the vision of the occultist is the same as leaders of AIM—to obtain all the powers Jesus had and usher in the kingdom of heaven on earth, where do the leaders of AIM stand? What gospel will World Racers bring with them on their mission trip?

CHRIST—THE ALCHEMIST?

Probably the most disturbing series of posts I read while researching AIM were written by Jeff Goins. One, which was entitled, "Mini-pilgrimages,"[65] left me stunned, and that's pretty hard to do. He wrote similar thoughts in a piece for Burnside Writers Collective entitled, "The Importance of Leaving Home."[66]

Using Richard Rohr once again as his mentor, Goins

compares the World Race to a pilgrimage—a *"journey of self-discovery."* He suggests leaving home helps World Racers to "experience the discovery process," and that they "are in a "lifelong process of journeying in God."[67]

Besides using the New Age theme of the journey of self-discovery and finding one's true self to describe the World Race, what else was so shocking? Richard Rohr wasn't the only author who denies the unique divinity of Jesus Christ Goins used to garnish his thoughts about pilgrimage. At the end of both articles, he recommends reading *The Alchemist*, a modern-day fable written by well-known, practicing Brazilian occultist, Paul Coelho. Why would he do so? Because Goins believes *this* book would help World Racers "find out more about pilgrimage."

You will find the practice of alchemy in books of sorcery and in the books of Jewish mysticism, the Cabala. Paul Coelho calls himself "a wizard" and admits to having dabbled in black magic. It was reported that he was influenced by Aleister Crowley, probably the most recognized occultist of the 20th century. Coelho claims, however, that he gave up "black magic" after he dealt "with forces" he "was not familiar with and with total irresponsibility."[68]

The main character in *The Alchemist* is a shepherd boy named Santiago who, Coelho points out, studied theology and attended seminary but didn't believe he could find God there. Santiago spends the night in an abandoned church, and having the same dream he had a week before, decides to visit an old gypsy woman who could interpret dreams. The gypsy explains "dreams are the language of God."[69] After listening intently to Santiago's dream, she tells him that he must go to the Pyramids in Egypt to find his "treasure."

Before Santiago embarks on his journey, he meets an old man who can read his thoughts. The man introduces himself as

Melchizedek, the king of Salem, and tells Santiago that his mission on earth is to realize his "Personal Legend." The boy finds out Melchizedek is an alchemist and is told an alchemist "understands the forces of nature" and wants to show "his extraordinary powers."[70] [Note: In both the Old and New Testament, Melchizedek is seen as a prefiguration of Jesus or type of Christ (Genesis 14:18; Psalm 110:4; Hebrews 7). This blasphemous comparison leaves the impression that our Lord and Savior, Jesus Christ, is a sorcerer.]

Dreams and omens help guide Santiago on his *mission adventure* into the world of alchemy, danger and love. Towards the end of his fable, author Paul Coelho writes:

> The boy reached through to the Soul of the World, and saw that it was a part of the Soul of God. And he saw that the Soul of God was his own soul. And that he, a boy, could perform miracles...
>
> The men were terrified at his [the boy's-cvk] sorcery. But there were two people who were smiling: the alchemist, because he had found his perfect disciple, and the chief, because that disciple had understood the glory of God.[71]

Did the boy *really* understand the glory of God, or something else? The ancient, occult art of alchemy, known as the magical craft of the Black Country (Northern Egypt and the Nile Delta), is both a physical science and a mystical, spiritual journey. In its physical science aspect, alchemy is based on the Egyptian belief that certain alloys contained magical powers that could turn lead into gold. Beside their efforts at turning led into gold, alchemists also searched for an elixir that would bring immortality to those who learned its secrets, and tried to create life artificially. They "based their study primarily upon direct, personal revelation through visions and dreams."[72]

In its spiritual aspect, alchemy is a metaphor for spiritual transformation, a source of *esoteric* thought. Like lead turning into gold, the "imperfect person, leaden and dark, could become pure and golden through a gradual process leading to spiritual illumination."[73] This brings about a transformation of consciousness, which is called, *authentic spirituality.*

Magical/occult practices are used not only to turn lead into gold, but to turn man into god equipped with all the powers Jesus had. The *journey* or *pilgrimage* is a spiritual quest for knowledge, which sounds innocent enough, until you understand how the knowledge is obtained and what the knowledge is.

I found *The Alchemist* in the metaphysical section at Borders, along with two other fictional works of Coelho's, *Brida* and *The Witch to Portobello.* These two books, especially Brida, are full-blown, blatant endorsements of witchcraft and its pagan Goddess religion. In *Brida,* a young Irish girl named Brida, searches for someone to teach her the art of magic and other esoteric/occult arts. She finds a magician named Magus and then a character, appropriately named Wicca, who teaches her the Tradition of the Moon, etc. I won't go into anymore, suffice it to say, through his "fiction," Coelho leads his readers deep into the *real* world of the occult. India's most prominent Wiccan (practicing witch), Ipsita Roy Chakraverti, believes Coelho borrowed the name Brida (or Bridgette) from the Irish goddess of Wicca who symbolizes the transformation of the soul.[74]

Why would an AIM staffer, a "missionary," want to lead *anyone* to Coelho's works? These three books were bad enough, but what I found next in between Coelho's many works of fiction proved to be more disconcerting. It was the personal account of his own journey of "self-discovery," interestingly entitled, *The Pilgrimage. The Alchemist* and *The Pilgrimage* go together. As it states on the back-cover of *The*

Pilgrimage: "In many ways, these two volumes are companions—to truly comprehend one, you must read the other."[75]

Between these two books, you'll learn the importance of breathing exercises, visualization techniques and contacting spirit guides. You will read of Coelho's love for magic, alchemy, get a very twisted view of God, and a whole lot more. Because I believe it's critical to understanding the possible ramifications of having anyone getting involved with AIM and learning the practice of contemplative/listening prayer, I'm going to provide a sample of what is found in *The Pilgrimage*.

In *The Pilgrimage*, Coelho writes of his involvement with the esoteric, mystical Order of Ram. Throughout the book, he is taught how to do different "Ram exercises" that are essential to his "journey." Relaxation, deep breathing exercises, and visualization help him contact his spirit guide. Coelho reveals: "Through my experiences with the Tradition [occultism-cvk], I had already communicated with many spirits. I was absolutely certain that there was a life after death, but it had never occurred to me to wonder just how the transition was made."[76] One Ram exercise, called "The Buried Alive Exercise," almost had me gasping for air.

You will travel with Coelho to the initiation of a man into the secretive order of the Knight's Templar. A ritual is performed in which a circle is drawn around the men for protection as the High Priest invokes "the King" who rules over "the Infernal Order of the Dominion of the East." Then Coehlo recalls:

> A profound silence followed, and even without being able to see him, we could sense the presence of the being who had been the object of the invocation. This was the consecration of the ritual, a propitious sign that we should continue with our

magical activities...

> The High Priest sprinkled water over us without stepping into the circle. Then, with the sacred ink, he wrote in the earth the seventy-two names by which God is known within the Tradition.

> All of us—pilgrims and Knights—began to recite the sacred names. The flames of the torches crackled, a sign that the spirit that had been invoked had surrendered.[77]

What happens next is chilling. Dancing within the circle, Coelho begins to enter "into a powerful state of ecstasy." He thinks he sees the "face of Ram" but finds, "it was only the face of N., the spirit that had been invoked, who was well known to me." At this point, Coelho says he was in a trance, but when the voice of the High Priest called out, his trance was broken. The High Priest speaks to the spirit and commands him to depart only to return when he is "conjured by the sacred rites of the Tradition."[78]

This is supposedly done in the *light* of God's love!

Towards the end of the story of his pilgrimage, Coelho redefines the meaning of Jesus' work on the cross, the atonement. Pay close attention to what he says, as it exposes the way leaders in the Emergent movement and in Charismatic/Pentecostal streams are redefining it today.

In Esoteric Christianity, the suffering and sacrifice of Jesus models the sacrifice and suffering we should expect along our own journey of self-discovery. Jesus was the way-shower to what we all can become. Coelho exemplifies this when he writes:

> "My Lord," I said, finally able to pray, "I am not

nailed to this cross, nor do I see you there.

The cross is empty, and that is how it should stay forever; the time of death is already past, and *a god is now reborn within me.* This cross is the symbol of the infinite power that each of us has. *Now this power is reborn, the world is saved, and I am able to perform your miracles, because I trod the Road of the common people and, in mingling with them, found your secret. You came among us to teach us all that we were capable of becoming, and we did not want to accept this. You showed us that the power and the glory were within every person's reach, and this sudden vision of our capacity was too much for us. We crucified you, not because we were ungrateful to the Son of God but because we were fearful of accepting our own capacity...*

I have walked so many miles to discover things I already knew, things that all of us know but that are so hard to accept. Is there anything harder for us, my Lord, that discovering that we can achieve the power?[79]

Here, Coelho is saying that through sacrifice and suffering (our death), we find our true self. As he explains a couple of pages later: "A god sleeping within me was awakening."[80] It is this awakening within each one of us that will save the world. In his vision, Coelho sees "the lamb" and things that "were reminiscent" of the Apocalypse. Everything ended "with every human bring on earth awakening the sleeping God and all of God's power."[81]

Coelho's vision is found in ancient Eastern/occultic mysticism which holds ties to Hinduism, Buddhism, Gnosticism, witchcraft, sorcery, Native American shamanism, the books of Jewish mysticism (the Kabbalah, or Cabala) and all other occult systems. We are seeing a revival of Babylonian, Indian, Chaldean, Sumerian, Egyptian and Persian beliefs and practices God condemned.

Following Paul Coehlo's cue that we are "capable of becoming," Jeff Goins sees that the pilgrimage is "as much about leaving as it is about *becoming.*"[82] A word often used in esoteric thought, "becoming" describes the evolutionary process of one's growth into godhood.

Could Goins' series on pilgrimages and his promotion of *The Alchemist* be just a coincidence? I don't believe so. The more subtle works of Richard Rohr and blatant occult works such as alchemy, have precisely the same core esoteric teaching. Hidden underneath occultism's "Christian" veneer is the same lie Satan used to deceive Eve, "you will be like God" (Genesis 3:5). It makes perfect sense.

Goins' post, "The Importance of Leaving Home," got some attention. One responder named Aart wrote: "I'm also a big Paulo Coelho fan and I don't know if you have heard about his blog http://www.paulcoelhoblog.com. I started as a fan and now I'm collaborating with him and thought that you would like to enter his universe. Check out the blog, if you want, or subscribe to his newsletter [leaves address-cvk]. You'll see a community of *warriors of light* sharing ideas, dreams and most importantly *following their personal legend...*"[83]

Will World Racers be warriors of light? Thousands of young adults are being influenced by "missionaries" who have gleaned their truth from occult sources. You can't do so without serious consequence. They will be "judged more strictly" (James 3:1).

THE HERO'S ADVENTURE—COMPARING THE GOSPELS TO HARRY POTTER

Equally disturbing was Jeff Goins' comparison of the Gospels with the Harry Potter series, the Star Wars series, and Donald Miller's *Through Painted Deserts.* Goins insists: "They are all stories of people becoming heroes by leaving home. All of those stories include risk and danger. They require sacrifice. This is the cost of a truly great story."[84] His analogy is more in tune with something you would read in the chapter entitled, "The Hero's Adventure," out of the New Age favorite by Joseph Campbell, *The Power of Myth,* or something from Campbell's famous work, *A Hero With a Thousand Faces,* rather than anything you'd find in Scripture. [Note: After writing this, I found a post by Seth Barnes, "You can be a hero" (10/29/2009), describing the hero's journey. In it he says: "Typically the hero's life is framed as a journey. *Joseph Campbell describes it in his book The Hero with a Thousand Faces.*"][85]

Why would a man involved in missions recommend *The Alchemist* for reading and compare Harry Potter and Jesus with becoming heroes? Should what our Savior accomplished be compared to the accomplishments of Harry Potter, a sorcerer? You can understand why Goins used emerging mystic Donald Miller for comparison, but using blatant occultism shows a much deeper problem.

A LUCIFERIC INITIATION?

In "So Beautiful by Len Sweet and Other Free books," (5/4/2009), Jeff Goins gives his tacit endorsement of Emergent author, Leonard Sweet. He also provides "a glimpse at *So Beautiful*" for his readers. In this "glimpse," Sweet is called the "Good Doctor" and it's stated:

So Beautiful unearths God's deep-rooted dreams for

the church after his own heart. Recommended for missional, organic, and house church provocateurs, as well as open-minded church folks.[86]

If Sweet is a "Good Doctor," I'd hate to see who Goins would call a bad one. Sweet's New Age pleaser, *Quantum Spirituality*, and two of his other works, *Soul Tsunami* and *AquaChurch*, are leading many, like Goins, into the dark world of the occult. In *Quantum Spirituality*, probably one of the most deceptive books I've read, Sweet praises well-known Luciferian and New Age leader, David Spangler. "I am grateful to David Spangler for his help in formulating this "new cell" understanding of New Light leadership,"[87] writes Sweet.

If Spangler is considered by Sweet and other Emergent leaders to be a "New Light" leader, could the *initiation* Spangler writes about in his work, *Reflections on the Christ*, be the initiation Barnes and Goins say is needed? I'm not sure, but the "coincidence" is too serious to ignore. In *Reflections on the Christ*, Spangler, who channels a disembodied spirit guide named John, declares "Christ is the same force as Lucifer" and reveals his belief that "Lucifer is literally the angel of experience."[88] Seeing the importance of initiation to Barnes, Goins and Richard Rohr, and seeing the importance of initiation in Coelho's works, what David Spangler prophecies next should be taken as a solemn warning to those about to go on the World Race:

> Lucifer comes to give to us the final gift of wholeness. If we accept it then he is free and we are free. That is the Luciferic initiation. It is one that many people now, and in the days ahead, will be facing, for it is an initiation into the New Age.[89]

CELTIC SPIRITUALITY & ANAMCHARA

Revealing the depth to which occultism has played in the life of AIM's founder, in his post, "Spiritual direction: advice from a soul friend" (9/14/007), Seth Barnes writes of the importance of having an "anamchara," a soul friend.[90] What he says in his post would sound harmless enough to those who don't know anything about Celtic spirituality, but at the end of his post he adds: "Read more here on Celtic Spirituality," and provides the link to All Saints Parish: Celtic Spirituality.[91] When you click it on, Celtic music beings to play. You'll see a picture of a Celtic cross and a brief outline of the beliefs found in Celtic spirituality. Links are provided for those who wish to learn more about the Celtic tradition, their prayers, and saints.

I clicked on the Feast of Samhain (All Hallow's Eve/Halloween), the "most important of the ancient Celtic feasts," and received a good education on the pagan background of the Celts and Halloween. Though, the fact that this is also the Witches' Sabbat was left out. Among other things, I learned that "the most magically potent time of Samhain was at night." Many rituals were used during this "very holy time" when "the dead could return to the places where they had lived." "Celts put out food and drink for the dead with great ceremony, and left their windows, doors, and gates unlocked to give the dead free passage into their homes." "Swarms of spirits," were said to pour into their world on November Eve, "but not all of these spirits were friendly." "Celts carved the images of spirit-guardians onto turnips and set these 'jackolanterns' before their doors to keep out unwelcome visitors from the Otherworld." Divination to foretell the future was practiced using hazelnuts, symbols of wisdom. A great bon-fire was made and "after being ritually devoted to the gods in pagan times," cattle were slaughtered for sacrifice. "Personal prayers in the form of objects symbolizing the wishes of supplicants or ailments to be healed were cast into the fire."[92]

It's explained that with the rise of Christianity, Samhain

was changed into All Saint's Day, "to commemorate the souls of the blessed dead who had been canonized that year." The history lesson ends with the merging of paganism and Christianity: "Throughout the centuries, pagan and Christian beliefs intertwine in a gallimaufry (hodgepodge) of celebrations from October 31st through November 5th, all of which appear both to challenge the ascendancy of the dark and to revel in its mystery." At the bottom of the page, you'll see a picture of a face, or mask, with oak leaves coming out of it. (The oak is regarded as the most sacred of all trees to the Celts who believe trees to be passageways to the otherworlds of spirits and messengers to the gods.) A "Chant for Samhain" is then provided for you to say. [93]

Desiring to find out a bit more of what Barnes could possibly be leading his readers to, I clicked on "Shape-Shifting Meditation." For some reason, thoughts of Harry Potter entered my mind. In this monistic/pantheistic (all is One, all is God) nonsense, the author of this meditation takes you on a guided imagery tour. "Close your eyes, and send your consciousness down through the room...down, deep down, into the earth....Let your consciousness become one with the mineral kingdom...the stone people are alive, it's just that their hearts beat slower than ours."[94] You are then guided to "become one" with the plant kingdom, the animal kingdom, and finally, back to the human kingdom. The occult practice of "shape-shifting" was "an integral part of Celtic shamanic experience."[95]

The paganism found in historic Celtic Spirituality has hardly been taken out of it. Researching the word, "anamchara," you find yourself entering into the world of Celtic mysticism. The objective of the anamchara is that of being a mentor—someone to help a person along their journey in finding God. They aren't suppose to instruct you in sound doctrine, or necessarily the Scriptures, but rather guide you along the path you desire to know "God."

The idea of an anamchara can be traced back to the Druids and shamans and was continued through the "Christian" saints and mystics. Druids, the high priests of the Celts, saw themselves as gods, believed in reincarnation, practiced divination, cast spells, and performed human sacrifice. Druids still gather around Stonehenge today performing rituals, chanting, and entering into altered states of consciousness.

In her fictional work, *An Acceptable Time*, the late Madeleine L'Engle, who is highly acclaimed in Christian circles as a "wonderful, Christian" author, likened Christ to a Druid. It's quite similar to the way in which Coelho equates Melchizedek with being an alchemist. L'Engle's influence within Christian churches and schools can hardly be exaggerated. I've seen the tragic results and documented them in my book, *Battle to Destroy Truth: Unveiling a Trail of Deception.*[96] I was also a contributing writer and researcher for *Trojan Horse: How the New Age Movement Infiltrates the Church* by Samantha Smith and Brenda Scott. Both of these works expose her numerous occult ties, the occult beliefs and practices she endorses as "Christian," and the blasphemous ways in which she purposefully distorts the gospel.[97]

It was hard for me to read Jeff Goins defense of L'Engle against those who discerned her fictional and non-fictional writings, as well as the countless speeches she gave: "Either there is room in the family of God for creative types like C. S. Lewis, Madeleine L'Engle, Paul Young, you and even me, or we're all heretics. Sorry, but I don't buy the latter option."[98] He needs to reconsider his options.

THE PARENTS' GUIDE

Keep in mind all the information you have read so far. Then, think about the objective of AIM—"to throw over-protected youth out into the world to formulate their own worldview..." I believe the parents who accused AIM of being a cult may have had good reason to be concerned. Why would a mission team have to prohibit or limit communication with the family? While the Bible teaches a child to honor their mother and father and to hold on to what they've been taught concerning the Scriptures (2 Timothy 3:12-16), this organization seems to be saying just the opposite.

The "Parents' Guide" is, to say the least, troubling, if not downright infuriating. Reading the handbook, as well as several other articles on the importance of being part of the World Race, I felt I was being told that my child was now in the hands of experts who would help undo all the bad parenting I did. AIM staffers would be there to "mature" *my* child in *their* path to know God. The guide explains: "'Initiation' is the process used for the radical discipleship we practice."[99] The process of "initiation" involves abandonment, brokenness, dependence, empowerment, calling, and finally, confirmation. **"We are placing a demand on them to mature and take their rightful places as heirs of His Kingdom. Even though this may be scary to them, we believe it is necessary.**"[100]

While AIM staffers and like-minded coaches help the "over-protected" child form his own worldview, parents are told that their child must go through a feeling of "brokenness" and "start the treacherous journey of leaving behind belief systems defined by others."[101]Using Genesis 12:1, where the Lord says, "get out of your country, from your family, and from your father's house, to a land that I will show you," they misleadingly compare Abraham's call to go to the Promised Land to the mission World Racers are on:

> The journey from the familiar is imperative to this goal: they must journey away from the guidance of family, the security of friends and the predictability of their everyday lives. *They must learn to rely on*

their own pursuit of the things of God and not live a life where they are spoon-fed their worldview and theologies.[102]

Parents are also informed that the process of "abandonment" and "brokenness" are necessary for the "transition" their child must go through "to pursue their own pathway of faith toward God." **Communication to parents, family and friends is limited and discouraged**:

> There will be times when we ask them to fully abandon and not be tied to facebook, skype and other means of communicating back home. We desire for them to move past the stage of abandonment and into empowerment, calling and confirmation, but first they may walk through times of limited communication and what may seem like silence from the field. Racers are encouraged NOT to carry cell phones on the field.[103]

At the same time, parents are warned: "*Imputed trust must be exercised toward the World Race staff.*"[104] "Coaches," (a set of parents who have a personal relationship with the World Race staff and leadership), are also provided for each "squad." "Coaches travel to the field a minimum of five times during the course of the World Race and spend 5-6 days at a time processing the experience with the racers and the teams in an effort *to guide the process to the ends we have established.*"[105] What are those ends? AIM leaders believe: "The time for childhood has passed and *if they are to change the world, they must change themselves. When they do, God's Kingdom will truly come.*"[106]

Before leaving the country, the World Racer must go through "a week of intense preparation" at a "training camp" and then another week of launch training once they're in the field. Ministry skills will be taught as well as skills in communication and learning how to dress and eat. Looking at the problems of human suffering (i.e. AIDS, human trafficking, etc.) is part of the training as well.

Some of the questions that will be asked by their trainers are:
1. What is the Gospel?
2. How can relationships open doors to introducing people to Christ?
3. How will the Spirit of God lead us to these opportunities?
4. Who are you?
5. Who does God intend you to be?
6. How has your journey brought you here?
7. What does a God-centered community look like?[107]

Finally, as these young people look "at the final expansion" of their world, they will "begin to discuss the Kingdom of God" with the staffers.[108]

While it's true to some extent that, as the "Parents' Guide" states, "their faith must become their own through trial and questioning," it seems AIM leaders feel *they* are the ones that need to teach young adults how to mature in the faith. The crucial question is—what gospel will be taught? Also, you can find many testimonials from previous World Racers in which they talk about being "broken" emotionally during their training. While one could say that it's good for them to feel the pain of those in Third World countries who are sick, hungry and poor (and it can be), there is plenty of evidence to suggest there is a whole lot more happening than meets the eye. The problem is, though racers have the opportunity of "stopping the process" and return home, how many will have the discernment and courage needed to do so once they're in the field? The weight of peer pressure and the guilt of leaving behind something they started out to accomplish may be too difficult to overcome.

Once the World Racer has been "broken," a new "dependence" on God is promised. Then comes "empowerment." Parents are told that God will start to "answer their prayers in ways they have never *experienced* before," and that he will "challenge them to believe and ask for more. And ultimately see the miraculous."[109]

EXPERIENCES OF RAISING PEOPLE FROM THE DEAD AND MORE

Seth Barnes assures these young, trusting, eager adults they can have all the powers Jesus had and have fun doing "the stuff." Stories of people having grown a leg longer to being raised from the dead have been reported by Seth Barnes. In one example, he relates a story of one of Heidi Baker's key leaders, Pastor Rego, who went to the house of a co-worker whose wife had died. Rego said he "started to feel strength and great power coming into me." He took the cover off the woman's head and began to pray. He prayed over an hour. She was still very cold. The second hour, he felt warmth coming into her. "I could feel her body warming up. I prayed all the way down her body. When I got down to her legs, the bottom of her legs were still cold. I picked her up, and then her eyes were open. She began to vomit and vomit. I can't even explain it....The third hour her whole body had movement. She was alive!"[110]

The account given by Pastor Rego sounds similar to that of a psychic healer or shaman rather than something we would see Jesus doing. When Jesus and the apostles raised the dead, it was instantaneous (John 11:38-43; Mark 5:38-43; Acts 20:9-12). He didn't have to "work" at it. If every believer is suppose to have all the powers Jesus has, why can't they do what Jesus did? So far, I haven't seen a post by Barnes claiming he or anyone else has raised someone from the dead four days after their death, instantaneously, like Jesus did for Lazarus.

The circumstances of this account are not provided by Barnes; he may not have had them himself. You don't know how long this woman was "dead," or if she was really dead at all. Her name isn't provided and the documentation to prove she was dead, probably doesn't exist. What bothers me most about the account given by Pastor Rego, is that you don't have a clue as to what *he* believes. I do know, watching Heidi Baker "soaking" in the Lord is both repulsive and sad. If you wish, click on this link: http://event.cbn.com/spiritualgifts/event/?EventID=11.[111] You will see Baker slide out of her chair onto the floor laughing hysterically when she's suppose to be speaking. Minutes into the video, she begins to make a strange purring laugh—or maybe she was rolling the letter r. Sometime later, she begins to cry. Others who are watching her come up seeking "the transference" of the Holy Spirit. People begin falling down, shaking and shouting. It looks more like madness than anything of the Holy Spirit. While there is no reference anywhere in Scripture to us being able to catch or transfer the Spirit in this way, you can find similar incidences watching Hindu practitioners of Kundalini Yoga, or Native American shamans in their trances.

At age 16, Baker was living on an Indian reservation and was "led to the Lord by a Navajo preacher." Does anyone know what that preacher believed? Several months later she "was taken up in a vision for several hours and heard the Lord speak to her and tell her to be a minister and a missionary to Africa, Asia and England."[112]

I firmly believe God gives us miracles today, but not in the way Benny Hinn, Heidi Baker, and other Charismatic "faith healers" claim. I doubt anyone reading Barnes' post involved with AIM ever questioned what gospel Heidi Baker or Pastor Rego believe. They need to do so. I've seen the damage done by attitudes of complacency and the foolishness of blind trust.

Back in 1994, I wrote an article entitled "New Hermeneutic or Ancient Wisdom?" for the *Christian Renewal*. It was a response refuting an article entitled, "Miracles and Healing," by Dr. John H. Boer, a missionary with Christian Reformed World Missions to Nigeria. In his article, which was printed in the Calvin Theological Seminary AlumNews, Boer equated the miracles Moses performed to those of the magicians. The only difference, he claimed, was that the magicians had used their power for oppression. Boer asserted these powers are found in nature and can be harnessed and controlled. He was describing the difference between white and black magic. I'm not sure if he even realized, or believed, God condemns both.

One World Racer was disappointed that she couldn't raise the dead *after only a week of being on the World Race.* Allen Boehm, another World Racer, prayed eight to nine hours for a man who had died from a respiratory illness to get up and walk. When he didn't see any results (with many people observing), he thought: *"Alright God, I want to give you a chance to glorify yourself."*[113]I wondered as I read this, if he even realized the utter audacity it took to say such a thing. The complete irreverence and arrogance shown in what this young man said seemed oblivious to him. Towards the end of his account, Boehm wrote that he learned God gets the glory regardless of the results, but he can't wait to try raising the dead again.

I went on several other blogs to find out what kind of impact the World Race had on participants' beliefs. Each one was more disheartening than the next. Erika Baldwin provided a list of different things she now *experiences* since going on the race. Here's a few she shared:

1. It has become normal to hear the sounds of Heavenly instruments playing wherever I go, all throughout the day.
2. It has become normal to hear angels harmonizing with us while we worship.
3. It has become normal to see armies of angels standing in front, behind, and on either side of us when we pray.
4. It has become normal to hear God's voice audibly.
5. It has become normal to pray in a Heavenly language [speaking in tongues-cvk].
6. It has become normal to weep uncontrollably over the things that grieve the Holy Spirit.
7. It has become normal to break out into side-splitting laughter with the joy of the Holy Spirit.
8. It has become normal to believe in AND TO SEE healing and deliverance [casting out demons-cvk].[114]

I wondered, after reading this, if Erika ever questioned the visions of angels she saw, or the miracles she claims to have witnessed. Since she can't test experience—something that is subjective, she was obviously going by what she was taught.

Another former World Racer wrote about the *experience* she had during a "silence fast" in her post: "The Silence: Day 2." Taking a quote from contemplative Henry Nouwen, she wrote:

It is this **nothingness** (in solitude) that I have to face in my solitude, a **nothingness** so dreadful that everything in me wants to run to my friends, my work, and my distractions so that I can forget my **nothingness** and make myself believe that I am worth something. The task is to persevere in my solitude, to stay in my cell until all my seductive visitors get tired of pounding on my door and leave me alone. The wisdom of the desert is that the confrontation with our own frightening **nothingness forces us to surrender** ourselves totally and unconditionally to the Lord Jesus Christ."[115]

On the second day of her silence fast, Kathryn thought: "Father, this silence fast is dumb. Now I want to avoid You, because I'm afraid to hear Your voice. I want to run to anything or anyone else to get away from feeling this way."

I wish she had run—as fast as her feet could take her. It makes me sick at heart to see so many young people being led astray by leaders who are rejecting the Truth and turning to another gospel.

Our children must learn to be like the Bereans who examined what Paul said daily against the Scriptures, and were commended for doing so (Acts 17:11). Still, these young, impressionable adults will be in the hands of people who will be teaching, training and "discipling" them for almost a year. It's crucial for parents to do their own research, find out what the leaders of this organization believe, and what practices they'll be using. Because, instead of *supporting* the biblical teachings parents have so lovingly and dutifully taught their children throughout their life, AIM leaders may very well be *undermining* what their children have learned. Whether the World Racer is living at home, or grown and married, parents always have the obligation before God to let their young adult know candidly, yet lovingly, what they think, and advise them accordingly. The final decision, of course, should be left up to them.

Paul's charge to Timothy is a reminder to all of us:

> In fact, everyone who wants to live a godly life in
> Christ Jesus will be persecuted, while evil men
> and impostors will go from bad to worse,
> deceiving and being deceived. But as for you,
> continue in what you have learned and have
> become convinced of, because you know those
> from whom you learned it, and how from infancy
> you have known the holy Scriptures, which are
> able to make you wise for salvation through faith
> in Christ Jesus. All Scripture is God-breathed and
> is useful for teaching, rebuking, correcting and
> training in righteousness, so that the man of God
> may be thoroughly equipped for every good work.
> (2 Timothy 3:12-16)

Many in the church today have forgotten or ignored Paul's instruction to Timothy. False teachers are rarely mentioned from the pulpit, if mentioned at all. The importance of holding to sound doctrine, which Paul vigorously and continuously encourages (cf. Titus 1:9; 1 Timothy 1:10; 2 Timothy 1:13; 2 Timothy 4:3), is downplayed or scorned. Unity is based on experience and beliefs are subject to change at any given moment. Yet, those who look down upon people for holding fast to sound doctrine have their own set of beliefs they cling to.

Paul warned the apostles for three years with earnestness and tears to be on their guard, to watch out for false teachers who would be in among the church like ravenous wolves ready to devour. They were to keep watch over themselves and the flock (Acts 20:28-31).

We have been forewarned that Satan will disguise himself as an angel of light and his servants as prophets of righteousness (2 Corinthians 11:13-14). Jesus scolded the church of Thyatira for tolerating false teachings of the prophetess Jezebel and "Satan's so-called deep secrets"—a reference to the Gnosticism invading the church today (Revelation 2:20-25). But Jesus commended the church of Ephesus for testing those who claimed to be apostles and found them false (Rev. 2:2). Each of us need to "test everything!" (1 Thessalonians 5:21).

Jesus couldn't have made the dangers of blind trust any clearer than this:

> Not everyone who says to me, "Lord, Lord," will enter the kingdom of heaven, but only he who does the will of my Father who is in heaven. Many will say to me on that day, "Lord, Lord, did we not prophesy in your name, and in your name drive out demons and perform many miracles?" Then I will tell them plainly, "I never knew you. Away from me, you evildoers!" (Matthew 7:21-23)

AIM's outreach to help the poor, the orphans, the disabled, and the sick in third world countries is noble. Trying to bring awareness of human trafficking and AIDS is commendable. Their *enthusiasm* for sharing the good news of "the kingdom of God" is to be applauded. But, it's been made crystal clear that doing good works won't save us: "For it is by grace you have been saved, through faith—and this not from yourselves, it is the gift of God—not by works, so that no one can boast. For we are God's workmanship, created in Christ Jesus to do good works, which God prepared in advance for us to do" (Ephesians 2:8-10). Good works should be evident in a Christian's life, but salvation can't be earned by keeping the law or doing good works. In fact, if we think they do, we are "under a curse" (Galatians 3:10). If anyone preaches a "different gospel," Paul cried, "let that person be eternally condemned!" (read Galatians 1:6-10).

I've talked with so many Christians who think the occult is something "out there," something blatant they will easily spot. They have absolutely no clue as to how deceptive it can be. By appealing to the ego, redefining Christian terminology, and undermining the unique authority of Scripture, the lies of Esoteric Christianity have infiltrated countless churches and mission fields as well. In her work, *Esoteric Christianity*, first published in 1901, Theosophist/occultist Annie Besant asks: "Is Christianity to survive as *the* religion of the West?" Her answer: "If it is to live, it must regain the knowledge it has lost, and again have its mystic and its occult teachings."[116]Her wish is rapidly coming true.

I am convinced Eastern/occultic mysticism is at the very heart of AIM. It's the reason Harry Potter can be compared with the Gospels and works by a practicing sorcerer can be recommended for reading. It explains why searching out Celtic Spirituality can be encouraged, and why contemplative/ listening prayer is endorsed and taught. I believe it's behind the reason why leaders of AIM think we can have all the powers Jesus had, why they separate Jesus from Christ, and why it is possible for them to proclaim we are "becoming God with skin on."

We have, dare I say it, "occultists" at the helm in so many churches and mission organizations that it seems unbelievable, except for the fact that we have been forewarned these things would take place. Rather than searching the Scriptures to interpret Scripture, these leaders have sought after those who are finding "truth" within their own imaginations, much like the Gnostics did in Paul's day. Instead of blaming the many injustices and atrocities found both within the church and society on our inherent sinful nature, they have forsaken the gospel and turned to the beliefs and "detestable practices" God condemns for their answers. The walls of Jerusalem were destroyed for that very reason (2 Chronicles 36:14-19).

I sent my niece and her parents much of the information I have given you. Unfortunately, it wasn't enough to change their minds. We recently found out that is was the youth pastor from their church who encouraged them to become involved with AIM. Because they prayed and then received all the money they needed for the trip, they believe it's God's will for them to go. You can now visit their own AIM blog website which also provides links to Seth Barnes' blog, the Wrecked for the Ordinary website, and other resources. The responsibility for doing so is grave, considering it may have eternal consequences not only for them, but for those they lead to AIM.

My husband and I first invited, then pleaded for all of them to come to our house and discuss these things. For whatever reason, they refused to do so. Instead, they contacted Seth Barnes, who, my niece said, put her mind at ease. I wasn't told the details of the conversations that took place through phone calls and e-mails, but another family member informed me that one of the questions my brother-in-law asked Barnes was about his endorsement of Richard Rohr. Apparently, in his defense, Barnes wrote a special blog post to answer him with. It's entitled, "Is all truth God's truth?" (November 12, 2010).[117]If you look it up, you'll find my response (under Claire), and other interesting ones as well.

I also wrote to Barnes about his provision of a video clip from Rob Bell's Nooma series on his post, "Everybody follows somebody, who do you follow?" (10/17/2007).[118]After doing so, I began to respond to posts by Jeff Goins hoping to get some positive reactions from readers and possibly from Goins and Barnes themselves. So far, there have been a couple of encouraging responses from readers, but Barnes and Goins are holding fast to what they've been teaching.

It is my hope that you will use this letter and supporting

documentation to expose what is taking place in mission organizations such as AIM. Please pray with me that eyes will be opened, especially for parents and the young adults who are so eager to travel the world, see and experience new, exciting things, and share their love for Jesus Christ.

Thanks so much for listening, Ingrid! May God bless your continued efforts in exposing the false teachings that are deceiving millions, seducing them into believing a whitewashed gospel that is utterly opposed to the Truth.

To Jesus Christ be the honor and glory!

Claris

P.S. Most of the documentation used are posts on Aim leaders' blogs. I didn't provide all the websites, but doing a search with the name of the author and title should bring them up. You can also see videos of the World Race training experiences and events like the Awakening in Ireland by doing just a bit of research. If you need additional information, please let me know!

CHAPTER TWO

MYSTICISM, MIRACLES & MAGIC: THE DECEPTION CONTINUES

> Anyone who pretends to be interested in magic or the occult for reasons other than gaining personal power is the worst kind of hypocrite...
>
> White magic is supposedly utilized only for good or unselfish purposes, and black magic, we are told, is used only for selfish or "evil" reasons. Satanism draws no such dividing line. Magic is magic, be it used to help or hinder.
>
> Anton LaVey, *The Satanic Bible*

Since my letter was posted online over four years ago, I have received many encouraging responses by caring and discerning Christians. Some who replied had a son, daughter, friend, or relative who were participants in the World Race. I was also heartened after receiving letters of support from World Racers themselves—disturbing as some of them were. Others who read my letter hadn't heard of Adventures in Missions before. They were appalled and saddened to learn that leaders of a missionary organization were embracing occult beliefs and practices and using the mission field to change the beliefs, attitudes and values of young adults.

Not unexpectedly, there were several groundless and rather sarcastic responses to the concerns I had listed in my letter by those involved with AIM. Jeff Goins, Director of Marketing for AIM, appealed to Matthew 18:15, softly scolding Ingrid Schlueter for posting my letter (and me, in turn, for writing it). This was his reply:

> It disheartens me that you would post this article without first confronting the people (including myself) that you accuse of heresy. I understand and respect your desire to defend orthodoxy but this seems to circumvent the clear command in scripture to first go to a brother or sister you believe to be in the wrong...Aim is a Gospel-centered, Christian mission organization with sound doctrine at the core of what we do. You can read our belief statement here: http://www.adventures.org/about/believe.asp.
>
> I would be happy to share with you more about why we do what we do and answer any questions you have regarding our theology.[1]

I had seen this misuse of Matthew 18 many times over the years, so I responded:

> Matthew 18:15 has absolutely nothing to do with statements made publicly, for all to see. Paul corrected Peter "in front of them all" so no one would be mislead (Galatians 2:14). For you to use Scripture in this way shows either a complete misunderstanding of the text, or a purposeful deflection off of what is being said. I can't judge your motive. I hope it's not the latter.

As one person acknowledged in response to Goins, a belief statement doesn't mean much. Anybody can write a belief statement, but that doesn't guarantee they're abiding by that statement. [2]

Further remarks by Goins revealed his answer was not even close to being genuine. Nor did he deny or repudiate any of the facts I presented, even though there were many who asked him to do so online. They asked so that all reading my letter could decide if there was anything amiss in what I had written; they wanted an honest discussion. He refused to do so and instead invited people to e-mail him to discuss it one on one (divide and conquer is the name of the game).

His answer, and responses from a couple of World Racers who agreed with him, were yet another strong indication that something is radically wrong with the leaders of AIM and in their training of young adults.

Seth Barnes did not reply to my letter online, but continued to write against "the critics" of listening prayer on his blog.[3] Meanwhile, the arrogance and deception in his posts and those of Jeff Goins and Michael Hindes, as well as other AIM staffers and participants in the World Race, became increasingly and disturbingly clear.

Claims of demonic spirits being exorcised, limbs being re-grown, people being raised from the dead, and other miraculous healings, continue to be reported by Barnes and others on the World Race. Most "miracles" seem to happen over a period of hours, days or weeks. He even related the incredible story of one person being raised from the dead—after three days![4]

I believe miracles happen, but I must question the validity of all such assertions. Unfortunately, the only way to verify Barnes' claims is to fly overseas and check them out for yourself, but that might not be enough to answer questions of authenticity. We know from Scripture that counterfeit miracles also exist. That's why it is of such critical importance to know who you are placing your trust in and what they believe!

Unlike those reported by Barnes, the miracles Jesus performed were instantaneous. We do find an instance or two where you could say the miracle was done in two stages (John 9:1-7; Mark 8:22-25). It wasn't as though Jesus couldn't heal in an instant if He wanted to. He chose another method for His own purposes. In almost all instances, He healed with a word, a touch; He didn't have to "work" at it. Jesus didn't *try* to heal a person and fail—like many so-called faith healers today.

There is one other observation I'd like to mention. Jesus never boasted about what He could do. He never indicated at all that His Father "loves to show off"—as Seth Barnes' leads his readers to believe in his post, "More dancing, laughter and healing" (3/9/12).[5] Jesus healed not only out of unmatched compassion for the sick, blind, crippled and downtrodden, but also to validate His deity and authority (John 20:30-31; Mark 2:1-13).

Another reason Jesus healed that seems to be overlooked by so many today, was clearly demonstrated by the young, dedicated pastor of the church my daughter's family is attending. During his excellent in-depth series on the book of Matthew, he rightly pointed out that *repentance* was Jesus' objective! He denounced whole cities after performing miracles in them because the people refused to repent and believe in who He was (Matthew 11:20-24).

Now, please let me share with you a few more recent, critical examples of why I believe this missionary organization could be detrimental to the spiritual health and welfare of young, maturing adults.

On March 2, 2011, just a few weeks after my letter had been posted on the web, Michael Hindes, director of the World Race, posted an article called, "Provoking Again." It perfectly illustrates the reason I am so concerned for young adults participating in the World Race, as well as those going on short mission trips. Hindes began his article saying:

> My goal in ministry has always been to challenge peoples' beliefs. I want to see if there is any way they could let go of their presuppositions and embrace a greater truth. Not necessarily my truth, but a new truth they haven't yet discovered. Sadly, most can't do this because they're so busy defending their hypotheses. I'm not sure where we got the idea that Christianity was about first learning, then defending our theology and doctrine.[6]

Complaining about the 20's something crowd he had spent several years with, Hindes said he was "very shocked, even dismayed by how much they're dug in already regarding their understanding of God." His job then, as he describes it, is being "an instigator" who tries to "deconstruct at least some of their presuppositions." Those presuppositions include "their views about the Spirit, the Word, His voice, the Kingdom, evangelism, discipleship," and "the real purpose" for our existence.[7]

There is nothing wrong with challenging young people with questions to see if they understand why they believe what they do and encourage them to search the Scriptures to find their answers. There is, however, one huge problem. Hindes admits he's "stopped looking for answers." Instead, he would much rather be "in hot pursuit of some great new questions." His true intentions reveal themselves in the way he describes a conversation with one young Christian:

> Recently, after having a conversation about the goal of Kingdom living, I actually had a 25 year old ask me if I believed in the virgin birth, the atoning sacrifice, Jesus' bodily resurrection, and our eternal

reward? There was no room in their mind for any "true believer" to think differently about anything they'd been taught in Bible College.

Needless to say, I walked away a little perplexed and deeply troubled. We keep teaching generations that they can know everything about God and that the book of revelation is closed - "that's it, God has said it all, it's all been written down, the great scholars have broken it all down for us to plainly see." All I can say is WTH (what the heck, of course)?[8]

There's a reason this discerning 25 year old had to ask Hindes to explain what he believes about the essentials of the Christian faith. The questions he asks have absolutely nothing to do with prompting people to diligently study the Scriptures so they can correctly handle the word of truth (2 Timothy 2:15). It seems to me his purpose is to undermine the uniquely inspired word of God and *change* what true Christians already believe (read 2 Timothy 3:10-17 a few times!).

Why do I believe this is so? Because, like Seth Barnes and Jeff Goins, Michael Hindes was reading mystic, Richard Rohr, and quotes him just a couple of paragraphs later. As you've already seen, Rohr *denies* the unique divinity of Jesus Christ and *rejects* his unique atoning sacrifice to save us from the wrath of God upon sin. Despite this, Hindes provides this misleading quote by Richard Rohr:

"Usually, God disciples us by making our self constructed world (read, beliefs) fall apart. Our personal salvation project must show itself to be almost totally wrong. The refusal to allow this falling apart is what creates legalism and religion."[9]

Tragically, many authors claiming to be Christians have

the uncanny ability to convince their readers that holding firm to the *essential* doctrines of the Christian faith is on par with the same form of legalism displayed by the Pharisees. While some wrongly overemphasize works at the expense of God's grace and burden people down with frivolous man-made laws, to cast all Christians who hold to sound doctrine in that light is going way too far. In essence, this would mean having to reject what the Bible teaches concerning the person and work of Jesus Christ in order to disassociate ourselves from the Pharisees!

What Hindes doesn't seem to realize (or perhaps doesn't want to admit), is that mystics like Richard Rohr and leaders of AIM are doing the very thing they accuse others of. Aren't they preaching a works-oriented salvation—a form of legalism? What else can you call having to do a myriad of spiritual disciplines in order to become "at-one with God" or some universal consciousness (the New Age twist of the substitutionary atonement)? Salvation inevitably becomes what you do, not what Jesus Christ did!

Once you have delved into the world of mystics, it's an easy step into the mystical, esoteric world of Magic.

A few weeks after Michael Hindes wrote "Provoking Again," Jeff Goins was proudly telling readers online that his wife gave him "the full Harry Potter series as a birthday present." I have no quibble with a young missionary's freedom to read what they wish, but I don't believe what he said next was very funny. He asked, "Is God trying to *tell* me something? Am I called me to a *wizard*?!"[10] Yes, this is the way he worded it. You didn't read it wrong. I think he probably meant to say, "Am I called to be a wizard?" But, who knows.

Considering Goins' fascination with mysticism and the occult and his continuing endorsement of self-professed occultist/sorcerer, Paul Coelho, it's not a stretch to believe he might actually be considering the idea that "God" is calling him to be a sorcerer or wizard. On a website page entitled, "Jeff Goins: Missionary, Marketer, Writer," Goins' favorite books are listed.[11] Number three (at that time) was *The Alchemist: A Fable About Following Your Dream* by Paulo Coelho. In reading my letter, you've already learned how this book, though fictional, teaches blatant occult beliefs and practices—the worst of which is man can become God. Listen to how this blasphemous work is being promoted on his page:

> Paul Coelho's enchanting novel has inspired a devoted following around the world, and this tenth anniversary edition, with a new introduction from the author, will only increase that following. This story, dazzling in its powerful simplicity and inspiring wisdom, is about an Andalusian shepherd boy named Santiago who travels from his homeland in Spain to the Egyptian desert in search of a treasure buried in the Pyramids.[12]

What "ancient wisdom" does alchemy inspire? The wisdom of the world God has made foolish (1 Corinthians 1:20-25). This sorcerer's following will increase, and Jeff Goins is but one of many "missionaries" who is helping that happen.

I would like to share with you a much deeper meaning of the word *Magic* that those of you who haven't studied the occult may not know. For occultists, Magic isn't about pulling a rabbit out of a hat or performing sleight of hand card tricks. Marion Weinstein, author of *Positive Magic, Ancient Metaphysical Techniques for Modern Lives*, defines magic "*as transformation—change—in accordance with natural law and brought about by art and will.*"[13]

She traces the roots of magic back "thousands of years,

predating Christianity, Judaism, and recorded history," then ascertains: "The Eleusynian Mysteries, the Egyptian Mystery schools, and the legendary culture of Atlantis grew out of these same roots." Weinstein explains that growing alongside monotheism, were the Magical traditions—the books of Jewish mysticism (the Caballah), Gnosticism, "ceremonial magic societies, *alchemy*, and astrology. *In all these magical studies, which are still with us today, one unifying theme emerges: the development of self.*"[14]

Weinstein believes you can give any name to the Power Source within you that aids your development: "Him or Her, Goddess, God, Power, Universal Energy, Mind, Spirit, Science, Nature, Reason, The Source, or The Force."[15] This is one reason why there is so much confusion within the church. When authors borrowing from the occult use the name God, rather than Nature or Energy to describe the power that transforms *the self* into *the Self* (god), a deceptive mixture of Christianity and Magic brews. In this bubbling pot, add occult meditation techniques under the name of contemplative, centering, or listening prayer, combine altered states of consciousness, a voice coming out of the imagination called God, and the power to do miracles, and what do you have?

Occult author, Gareth Knight, writes: "Magic today is a particular specialized branch of a vast range of learning and speculation known as the occult. Like magic, the occult falls between religion and science....Our study must also include alchemy, which was magic using the terminology of science."[16]

Knight notes that meditation creates deeper and higher levels of consciousness in which a person can, supposedly, attain a more direct approach to truth and reveal a higher reach of human nature. The goal of this type of meditation and the goal of Magic (in the "higher" sense), is to fulfill one's spiritual potential. This encompasses the ability to contact spirit guides (some call them guardian angels or Teachers), and perform miracles like Jesus did. In the following paragraph, Gareth Knight describes the difference between White and Black Magic. I am convinced his description perfectly illustrates what Seth Barnes and Jeff Goins are truly teaching, and what is really being utilized on the mission field today. Knight reveals:

> All techniques, like all technologies, can be put to good use or bad, and in our field of inquiry this constitutes a division of the subject into White Magic and Black. The former is a use of techniques of the imagination to expand consciousness and improve the common good; the latter is their use for selfish or squalid ends. In the former people are healed or helped, in the latter they may be cheated, dominated or degraded.[17]

Once a person willingly decides to plunge deeper into the world of magic, mysticism and the occult, the ego can quickly take over.

Just one day after Michael Hindes posted "Provoking Again" on his blog, Seth Barnes posted a piece he had written called, "What permission do you need?" He suggests "a whole generation of young adults needs four kinds of permission if they are ever to grow into their potential." They need permission to come aboard, permission to dream God's dream of setting a broken world right again, permission to fail, and finally, permission to succeed. He assures his followers they are all children of the king and citizens of the kingdom, then invites (or commands) them to "join the tribe."[18]

I almost choked on my coffee when I got to the bottom of his page. Barnes tells the young people reading his post who look to him for spiritual guidance that they should "remember what Marianne Williamson wrote"—as if they knew who she is (and maybe, some do). He concluded his post with a poem written by this well-known New Age teacher which, I surmised, was to be useful for reminding them who they really are, help them attain their full potential, and "set a broken world right again."[19] In doing so, he betrays Jesus Christ once again, and leads a countless number of young adults into something so insidious, they wouldn't even begin to wrap their minds around the reality of it.

Marianne Williamson, a good friend of New Age queen, Oprah Winfrey, teaches *A Course in Miracles,* a New Age "bible" that was supposedly dictated by Jesus through medium Helen Schucman, an assistant professor of psychology at Columbia University's College of Physicians and Surgeons. *A Course in Miracles* is said to resemble the Hindu Vedas. Schucman's "Jesus" claims it is a "course in mind training."[20]

Williamson has been working alongside New Age medium, Barbara Marx Hubbard (who claims to channel "Christ"), petitioning the United States government to create a Department of Peace for the purpose of advancing their New Age agenda. Their goal is to bring in a one-world order and one-world spirituality. In order for this to become reality, everyone, they believe, must have a transformation of consciousness (become their Higher Self), resulting in a full planetary transformation of consciousness. This will, according to New Age ideology, create a unified, peaceful world.

The future, however, will not be very bright for those who refuse to embrace this new message of salvation. And, I doubt it will be peaceful. Through her "Christ," Hubbard proclaims those who refuse to evolve in their thinking—enough to accept a global spirituality, are a "lethal cancer" to the rest of humanity.[21]

Other high-ranking New Age and TV personalities are

beginning to follow Hubbard's lead, insinuating that death and/or being sent to "re-education" camps is inevitable to those who refuse to join their mission. But, don't be alarmed. Hubbard says (through her spirit guide), that they (we) will just be going through "God's purification process"—on another planet in the solar system! (Yes, I believe Hubbard's mind has been totally warped from using occult meditation and listening to the voice of her demonic "Christ.")

Perhaps a belief in reincarnation eases her mind at the thought of Christians being "purified" (slaughtered?). "Christ," through Hubbard, proclaims:

> Those of you undergoing the second death will be resurrected when you choose to become God-loving, but not among your brethren of the evolved humanity. You will go to God's school elsewhere in this universe, free to learn without the environment of fear. There are schools within schools for every soul I have ever created."[22]

When you understand the depth of darkness in Hubbard's prophesies, her close relationship with Marianne Williamson is very troubling. Of greater concern is the question of why Seth Barnes points readers in Williamson's direction. What does *he* know that his readers may not? And, what is she teaching through the poem Barnes chose to quote?

First, I'm going to provide you with Williamson's poem Barnes' posted on his blog. Then, I'm going to quote a teaching taken from *A Course in Miracles.* Read each closely and remember, Williamson teaches *A Course in Miracles.*

Our Deepest Fear
(by Marianne Williamson)

Our deepest fear is not that we are inadequate.

Our deepest fear is that we are powerful beyond measure.
It is our light, not our darkness, that most frightens us.
We ask ourselves, Who am I to be brilliant, gorgeous, handsome, talented and fabulous?

Actually, who are you not to be?
You, are a child of God.

Your playing small does not serve the world.
There is nothing enlightened about shrinking so that other people won't feel insecure around you.
We are all meant to shine, as children do.

You can check out this quote at the following website to see its connection with *A Course in Miracles*: <http://skdesigns.com/internet/articles/quotes/williamson/our_deepest_fear/>.[23]

Notice the build up of a person's self-esteem (ego)? Notice how she changes what a person is afraid of—not their "darkness" (you could say, sin), but their light? Who does Williamson believe all people are meant to be? Here's what she teaches from *A Course in Miracles*:

The name of Jesus is the name of one who was a man but saw the face of Christ in all his brothers and remembered God. So he became identified with Christ, a man no longer, but at one with God....Jesus remains a Savior because he saw the false without accepting it as true. And Christ needed his form that He might appear to men and save them from their own illusions....

Jesus became what all of you must be. He led the way for you to follow him. He leads you back to God because he saw the road before him, and he followed it. He made a clear distinction, still obscure to you, between the false and true. He offered you a final demonstration that it is impossible to kill God's Son; nor can his life in any way be changed by sin and evil, malice, fear or death...Is he the Christ? O yes, along with you.[24]

Marianne Williamson's light is darkness and darkness is her light (see Isaiah 5:20). She didn't find the wonderful hope Christians have because of Jesus Christ by searching the Scriptures. Williamson sought out her "happiness" in quite a different world. In her book, *Everyday Grace: Having Hope, Finding Forgiveness, and Making Miracles*, which she says "is for those who seek to work miracles," Williamson draws her thirsting readers into the world of mystics, mysticism and magic that she was lured into as a child:

I realize now that the journey, which started in my childhood—beginning with books about magic, then moving on to philosophy classes, astrology, tarot, the I Ching, and ultimately more classical theological studies and *A Course in Miracles*...has been a fairly common version of my generation's spiritual journey.[25]

She grew up, much like I did, in the 1960'and 1970's—the years that drove my parents just a little crazy. Those were the "hippie" years when young people were rebellious, high on drugs, transcendental meditation, "love," and, while on their tiptoes by the tulips, singing their theme song, Age of Aquarius. I didn't realize at that time, this rather fun song represented the dawning of the New Age—an age during which occultists hope to thoroughly wipe out true Christianity. Thankfully, by God's grace and devoted Christian parents, I escaped that world of illusion. It seems leaders of AIM, however, are bringing young people back to the time when the occult began to flourish.

Like Jeff Goins, Marianne Williamson's daughter is fascinated with Harry Potter (obviously, so is Marianne). She told her young child:

> Each of us has a mark on our forehead, just like Harry Potter, that speaks to the fact that all of us come from a very magical source.

> Harry Potter is one boy in a long line of mythical heroes who have reminded the human race that we are so much more than we think we are, much more powerful than we seem to know.[26]

Does this quote remind you at all of Revelation 13:11-16 where "the beast" forces everyone to take a mark on their right hand or forehead in order to buy and sell? I think the parallel is quite interesting. The striking absence of humbleness reminds me of the one prowling around like a roaring lion waiting for someone to devour (1 Peter 5:8).

"The mystic path," writes Williamson, "is a journey of personal transformation, and while the goal of the journey is to become our true selves, we can only do this by letting go of who we are not."[27] As in *A Course in Miracles*, she is saying that we must become Christs—along with Jesus.

Marianne Williamson was guest speaker for the "Be the Change" National Conference, held on March 17, 2012 in Maryland. Her subject: "Transforming Ourselves, Transforming Our World. She explored "the interface of personal and global transformation" and "the spheres of spirituality and social change."

Can you imagine the tremendous confusion leaders of AIM are creating in the minds of young adults who place their full trust in them to keep them safe from spiritual, emotional, and physical harm? What an utter shame! This feel good theology is being gobbled up like a box of mouth-watering chocolates by those craving love, acceptance and control. To have the power to perform the miraculous is merely bait—like a squiggly worm on a hook spotted by a hungry fish.

By reading hundreds of comments for over a year by World Race participants and staffers online, watching videos they have placed on You-Tube, reading their responses to posts by Seth Barnes, Jeff Goins, Michael Hinds and other AIM leaders, a Christian with their eyes wide open can see the hideous deception that is taking place. While not all World Racers may be affected by the teachings being thrust upon them, many have been.

During training camp, one World Racer noted on her blog that they learned to put a "God box" above their heads and followed these instructions: "**SMASH** IT TO THE GROUND! Say/Sing/Scream GOD I LET YOU OUT OF THIS BOX! And STAMP Jump DESTROY that box!" This, she writes, can be repeated "as many times as necessary" to remind them there are "NO LIMITATIONS" to the things they can do because they are now letting God out of the box. [28]

Another World Racer compared Jesus and his followers with Ted Turner's anti-Christian, earth-worshiping cartoon characters, Captain Planet and the Planeteers. The racer provides his readers with their chant: Earth. Fire. Wind. Water. Heart.—almost the exact same chant seen in books of witchcraft. He then explains though most people like the first four elements, he prefers the word "Heart." Why? Because it "...allows for one to speak to the inner spirit of animals and move them to help in situations or to warn them of danger. In a sense, you can hear the heartbeat of the nature around you."[29] Does this young World Racer know that he just described the Planeteers' occult belief of animism in which all of nature—trees, animals, rocks, etc., is inhabited with spirits?

Infusing occultism with Christianity, he continues by comparing the chant spoken by the Planeteers (to receive their power), to believers who are to "come together in unison, say words [pray-cvk], and let our Savior come down to the rescue." After quoting Jesus' words, "Where two or more are gathered in my name, there I am also," he shouts, "Awesome!" He quotes the Earth. Fire. Wind. Water. Heart. chant once more and finishes with the most haughty, blasphemous pronouncement: "'By your powers combined...I am the I AM!!'"[30]

Robby Riggs, yet another young adult who began an adventure with the World Race, studied for a time at the G42 Leadership Academy in Mijas, Spain. In 2011, he moved to Georgia to work full time with Adventures in Missions as overseer of the Ambassadors Program (14-18 year olds on Youth Mission Trips). In "Provoking Christ in Humanity" (5/13/2011), Riggs wrote:

> We all desire in our own ways to see Man come to know and understand their roles in the Kingdom of God here on earth as we continue to step in our own. All of us have come from different backgrounds, struggles, victories, and brokenness, but at the core *we are all walking more and more into Sons of God...*
>
> Let me say this: I believe you CAN provoke Christ in anyone! It is simply sharing with them your Father – your relationship with Him. Again, not religion but your Father who loves them deeply.[31]

I wonder if Robby Riggs understands that *only* Jesus Christ can be called the "Son of God" (singular, with a capital S)? I have not found the word "Sons" (capitalized and plural) anywhere in Scripture when referring to believers. I have, however, seen the term "Sons of God" used before. You will find it throughout *A Course in Miracles* and other New Age/occult literature. In *A Course,* readers are at times referred to as "Sons of God," or singularly, as a "Son of God. "

In *Everyday Grace,* Marianne Williamson clearly defines what Robby Riggs is actually saying: *"God did not create us individually, but as one; that is the esoteric [occult-cvk] meaning of 'only one begotten Son.'"*[32] Because those adhering to New Age thought believe Christ is the Christ-consciousness within all humanity, not the person Jesus from Nazareth, Williamson can say:

> It has been said that when the Buddha comes again, he will arrive not as a person but as a community. We will know that God is here on earth when we can see Him in one another.[33]

Your job in taking *A Course* is to become a Son of God, pure, holy and blameless so you can save yourself and change the world. When enough people join in this effort, "Christ's" vision is supposedly accomplished and heaven comes to earth. How can you do this? By listening to "God's" still, small voice in the silence—what Seth Barnes calls, Listening Prayer! As Williamson teaches:

> The more we pray, meditate, and take our spiritual practice seriously, the better listeners we become to the small, still voice for God. We come to understand that there are means of knowing beyond the rational.[34]

Seth Barnes continues to defend the practice of listening prayer against his "critics" on his blog. But, those who believe the Bible to be the final authority on all matters of faith and practice heed the words of the apostle John in Revelation 22:18-19:

I warn everyone who hears the words of the prophecy of this book. If anyone adds anything to them, God will add to him the plagues described in this book. And if anyone takes words away from this book of prophecy, God will take away from him his share in the tree of life and in the holy city, which are described in this book.

For Williamson, and for all those who follow her teachings, who is God? "He is the Mind of the realized Self."[35]

Is it any wonder *A Course in Miracles* is said to resemble the Hindu Vedas? The pantheistic (All is God) and monistic (All is One) beliefs found in Hinduism are unquestionably present. The God found in Scripture cannot be, in any way, Williamson's god, for God said: "I, even I, am the Lord, and apart from me there is no savior" (Isaiah 43:11). We are commanded by God not to have any other gods before him (Exodus 20:3-4).

The spiritual assault on young people working with Adventures in Missions—*under the alleged protection of its leaders*, is beyond comprehension. Reading a post by Adventures in Missions advocate, Mike Nagel, the deception that is being perpetrated upon them under the guise of working for God and His mission hit me hard once again.

Nagel acknowledges, quite enthusiastically, that he's "a Paul Coelho fan." After describing this sorcerer as "a pretty prolific blogger," Nagel quotes Coelho's post, "Yes, It is Worth It." The first sentence could have been taken straight out of *The Alchemist*: "Life is like a big bike race where the goal is to fulfill your personal legend." Coelho is making the point that fulfilling your personal legend has its challenges—loneliness, tiredness, monotony and doubts about one's own abilities, but in the end it's worth the effort. Nagel concludes:

In a bike race, the person who surges ahead to the finish might win money, temporary fame, or maybe just a yellow jersey. But in youth ministry, our prize is far greater. We are running this race, striving forward, to hear our Creator smile and say, "Well done, my good and faithful servant."[36]

Mike Nagel's words would have been so appropriate and encouraging, but his prior praise for Paul Coelho and *The Alchemist* make a mockery of Jesus' words, "Well done, my good and faithful servant" (Matthew 25:21).

Is a servant being faithful to Jesus if he leads others to what God has condemned, and consequently, another Christ? The authentic Jesus said:

Behold, I am coming soon! My reward is with me, and I will give to everyone according to what he has done. I am the Alpha and the Omega, the First and the Last, the Beginning and the End.

Blessed are those who wash their robes, that they may have the right to the tree of life and may go through the gates into the city. Outside are the dogs, those who practice magic arts, the sexually immoral, the murderers, the idolaters and everyone who loves and practices falsehood. (Revelation 22:12-15)

CHAPTER THREE

THE OCCULT SIGNIFICANCE BEHIND 11:11

And he [Jesus] said, "I tell you the truth, unless you change and become like little children, you will never enter the kingdom of heaven. Therefore, whoever humbles himself like this child is the greatest in the kingdom of heaven. And whoever welcomes a little child like this in my name welcomes me. But if anyone causes one of these little ones who believe in me to sin, it would be better for him to have a large millstone hung around his neck and to be drowned in the depths of the sea. Matthew 18:3-6

While you were reading my letter, did you ever wonder why the World Race consisted of going to 11 countries in 11 months? Knowing that the number 11 has a great deal of significance to occultists and the practice of numerology is common, the thought occurred to me that there might be a deeper reason why the number 11 had been chosen by Adventures in Missions.

I dismissed the notion entirely, until I came upon one racer's post called, "A World Race Manifesto?" (12-1-10). Sara Choe began as a participant in the World Race in 2008. In 2010, she joined the staff of Adventures in Missions as communications coordinator.

I was somewhat surprised that on Sara's post it was revealed many people have wondered, why 11? Then I found out. Perhaps unwittingly, she disclosed: "Those 11 months in a distinct combination of 11 countries has a specific purpose for each racer...a couple of upcoming Racers have touched on it."[1] Choe quotes racer, Emily Tuttle, a rather sweet-looking young woman:

> At training camp we talked a lot about the number 11. To most people, this number might seem random...
>
> We learned that the number 11 is very significant. Adventures in Missions didn't just roll a pair of dice, add up the numbers, and deploy their teams for that many months. The number 11 matters.
>
> Eleven is said to be the number of transition...that's code for change, right?...
>
> As training camp continued and I thought about this idea of transition and my aversion to change, I realized that the two words are not really synonyms. Change simply means moving away from the current state of things. Transition, however, implies a move toward something new.[2]

Transition was something this racer believed she needed in order to move towards the life God has for her and "the purpose to which He called" her.[3]

The other racer Choe mentions in her post shared "That change without transformation is intolerable...singing songs without worship is hollow...and having meetings without God showing up is pointless." The focus for all of them was on "experiencing God."

Words about change, transformation and transition, along with the emphasis on experience sounded all too familiar. There was no doubt left in my mind that these young adults were following their trainers' footsteps straight into the world of mysticism and the occult.

According to *Harper's Encyclopedia of Mystical and Paranormal Experience,* "The numbers 11, 22, and 33 are master numbers and are not reduced to single digits. People whose names correspond to these numbers are said to be highly developed spiritually."[4] Occultists claim the number 11 "is considered the path of spiritual awareness and knowledge beyond the grasp of others...It is also related to open-mindedness, intuition, idealism, and visions."[5]

Occultist/numerology buff, Simone M. Matthews, explained in her article, "2009: The Magic of a Universal '11' Year":

In numerology, the number 11 is a Master Number–'Master' meaning it is of intense/high vibrational frequency and *works within the etherical, magical and transcendental realms of creation.* Master numbers possess *great potential for learning and growth, and can bring major transformations in life.*

The number 11 is the most intuitive number and is a clear channel to the subconscious. It is the number of leadership, personal power and spiritual truths...

Matthews continued to say the "...vibrational 11 year is being powered by *visionary & humanitarian principles of change. Change for the greater good of all.*" They are all, "*pioneers of change.*"[6]

In her article, Matthews is describing the New Age goal of bringing in a new, socialistic one-world order and one-world spirituality through the transformation of each human being into their higher Self. Do *you* see much difference with the goal of Adventures in Missions?

I was rather dumbfounded when I found article after article by leaders of Prophetic ministries using the number 11 to say much the same thing—only in a slightly more "Christianized" way. In "2011 – A Year and Season of Great Transition for Everyone: HEARING God is Certain!" prophetess Carol Kelley wrote:

> For over a year now, the Lord has been speaking to me about transition. One of the ways He's done this has been through the number "11." I've lost track of the dozens even hundreds of times I've seen "elevens" - on clocks and thermometers, in dreams and visions, while reading the Bible, on the Internet and TV news, and even in the daily newspaper! God has used the number 11 to communicate to me that His promises are in the process of being fulfilled; in other words, "almost to completion" or "in transition."[7]

Listen once again to Simone Matthews:

> Have you ever noticed 11:11 all around you? On digital clocks, stereos, microwaves, DVD's posters, in nature etc. it is everywhere...'Jesus' in numerology breaks down to the number 11...[8]

Carol Kelley says she sought the Lord about what He might say to and through her about the year 2011. This "Lord" told her:

> "2011 will be a season of transition, not just for individuals, but also transition in ministries and in churches. I will move My people to the next level.

This will involve a relinquishment of expectations you have set for yourself. Be open to receive My expectations and directions for you!"[9]

Kelley continues her prophecy:

God indicated to me that in this coming transitional season, prophetic words and activity will increase and take on more importance in the life of His Church. Along with this, I feel urged to include a reminder that any Believer can hear the voice of the Holy Spirit, not just those with the gift of prophecy or office of prophet..."[10]

Her words reminded me of the World Race participant who said we had to quit putting God in a box; there are no limitations to what we can do.

Do a little research on the number 11:11 and you will come up with all kinds of strange articles. Many turning to numerology for guidance (knowingly or not), meditate, visualize and pray around the world at precisely 11:11 for the purpose of changing the world. But, who are they really praying to, and whose "kingdom" are they trying to bring in?

On one particular website, www.nvisible.com, an occultist named Solara provides you with an incredible amount of eye-opening information on the meaning of 11:11. But there is an article I would recommend reading instead, written by Synthia Esther. It's entitled, "Numerology Occult Magick – The Power Behind the Force." She researched the number 11:11 and found:

There is much psychic magick going on behind the scenes of the 11:11 numerical promptings. Such power is received and thus achieved by joint prayer in like group mind, ritual, dance, drumming, trance, visualization, meditation, and other Gnostic, shamanistic, ceremonial rituals of magick. Solara and facilitators of the 11:11 Gateway activations she promotes, are one such united force of occult magic.[11]

Esther not only provides critical information on 11:11, but gives a stirring testimony to the grace of God: "For we trust and depend on Jesus Christ, our Lord and Savior, to protect, guide, and lead us unto all truth, wisdom, and knowledge. His word, the Holy Bible, provides the answers to all our questions and problems in life."[12] (Note: Always discern and test what you read.)

I don't think it's necessary to provide you with more agonizing (yet informative) details in order to understand what is happening with Adventures in Missions and other missionary organizations who borrow from the occult.

CONCLUSION

God doesn't "show-off" his miracles, as Seth Barnes suggests, but Satan is more than happy to. If you crave the ability to perform miracles, hear "God's" voice and speak in tongues; if you desire above all else to *experience* being slain by the power of the Holy Spirit—be in a drunken stupor, roll over for hours in uncontrollable laughter, be glued to the floor for no apparent reason, howl like a wolf, or see beautiful visions of Jesus or angels, BEWARE! You may just get what you wish for, but it will *not* be of God. How can it be?

When listening to your intuition, exalting your imagination, and your experiences begin to over-ride sound doctrine, you are losing the battle, not winning the world. Doing good works will ultimately mean nothing if the true gospel is traded for "another gospel" and a slap on the back and exclamation of "well done!" causes one to compromise that old, old story which was "once for all entrusted to the saints" (Jude:3). Is this *really* worth it?

The emphasis on the greatness of performing miracles while praising those who deny Jesus Christ as the unique Son of God, is the ultimate betrayal of the only One who died so those who believe on Him may live.

The true Jesus warned His followers: "For false Christs and false prophets will appear and perform great signs and miracles to deceive even the elect – if that were possible. See, I have told you ahead of time" (Matthew 24:24-25).

For all of you reading this who love Jesus Christ with all of your heart, soul and mind, and wish to dedicate your life to Him, please bear in mind His prophetic words of caution. False teachings have no boundaries. Be loving, compassionate and trustworthy, but most of all, be true to the One who loves you beyond all measure. Remember:

> *This is the victory that has overcome the world, even our faith. Who is it that overcomes the world? Only he who believes that Jesus is the Son of God.* **(1 John 5:5)**

****

UPDATE

Besides *The Art of Listening Prayer*, Barnes' newer book, *Kingdom Journeys: Rediscovering the Lost Spiritual Disciplines* (2012), is recommended reading for World Racers to help them on their journey—their *process* of becoming. It is highly praised and endorsed by Richard Rohr, Emergent author, Frank Viola, and Dr. Ron Walborn, Dean of Alliance Theological Seminary and the College of Bible and Christian Ministry at Nyack College (New York). [Walborn is working together with Seth Barnes at times, speaking about spiritual formation and teaching World Racers the art of centering prayer (contemplative/listening prayer) during their training.][1]

As Barnes' title implies, listening prayer is promoted again in *Kingdom Journeys*. New Age mystic, Thomas Merton, Richard Rohr, and the pied piper of contemplative prayer, Richard Foster, author of *Celebration of Discipline* (1978), are used, supporting Barnes' lead into Eastern/occultic mysticism. At the conclusion of Chapter Six, "The Spiritual Act of Abandonment," Barnes quotes Merton: "Thomas Merton says there are seeds of grace flowing from God in every moment. Our only job is to present enough to receive them. God wants to connect spirit with body." What he neglected to point out is Merton's belief that we are all to become Christs. In his book, *New Seeds of Contemplation*, Merton, who combined Zen Buddhism with Christianity, writes:

It is the Spirit of God that must teach us Who Christ is and form Christ in us and transform us into other Christs. After all, transformation into Christ is not just an individual affair: there is only one Christ, not many. He is not divided. And for me to become Christ is to enter into the Life of the Whole Christ, the Mystical Body made up of the Head and the members, Christ and all who are incorporated in Him by His Spirit.[2]

Merton concludes, "In Christ, God became not only 'this' man, but also, in a broader and more mystical sense, yet no less truly, 'every man.'"[3]

In *Kingdom Journeys*, under the heading of "Dealing with Wet Blankets," once again, parents who have concerns about the World Race and discourage their young adult from going are made to look like they may very well be going against God's will if they try and keep them from such an important, mission adventure (i.e. kingdom journey, rite of passage, pilgrimage, initiation). Unfortunately, if the money comes in for the trip (now approximately $17,000.00 a person), many will think it is God's will if they don't research the organization and discern what they teach and practice.

Seth Barnes, who, as a friend pointed out, was on the team that developed the official U.S. Standards of Excellence in Short-Term Missions (STM) over a decade ago, continues to influence young adults after they participate in the World Race through his Center for Global Action (CGA). The Center…"is a realization of a lifelong dream of Seth's that people move from the initiation experience of a kingdom journey into an intentional time of discipleship to discover their calling."[4] Used for spiritual formation, the "goal of CGA is to help apprentices discover their identity and call in the kingdom of God."[5] As stated on the online FAQ's sheet, CGA "continues the growth process that begins in the World Race. Each applicant (Adventures in Missions alumni), will be evaluated by "past leaders, coaches, and team members." Housing and scholarships are available.[6]

With AIM's stated intent of "deconstructing 'The American Dream' and comparing it to 'The Gospel Dream,'" (Barnes' social gospel), Adventures in Missions began a program to create *sustainable* missional communities.[7] In the winter of 2012/2013, "those who put a year of their lives partnering with Adventures in Missions"—and "especially the 500+ annual graduate of "the Word Race,"[8] were given the opportunity to go to Spring Gate—"a training center whose goal is to create missional communities centered on food production." Located just outside Harrisburg, Pennsylvania, Spring Gate Vineyard & Farm is a 60 acre bucolic vineyard and farm to help people and their families learn about living in a "sustainable manner." The requirements and curriculum for this commune at that time, was "one year of discipleship by AIM prior to the start of the program that had to "include a significant portion of minimalist living."[9]

Is it mere coincidence that the United Nations is calling for "sustainable living" because of its belief in the so-called crisis of man-made global warming (or "climate change" when "warming" doesn't fit the criteria), and its anti-Christian, socialistic, utopian goal of a one-world government and one-world spirituality?

In July of 2012, Jeff Goins, who was raised in the suburbs of Chicago, Illinois, came out with his book, *Wrecked: When a Broken World Slams into your Comfortable Life*. It was published, unfortunately, by Moody Publishers—an arm of Moody Bible Institute in Chicago, Illinois, giving Goins an even wider audience in the Evangelical community. Worse, on Moody Radio, October 11, 2012, Chris Fabry interviewed Goins about his book on his show, Chris Fabry Live! – A Legacy of Faith // Wrecked. Of course, Adventures in

Missions was given a hearty endorsement during the interview as well.[10] Even more disturbing was the You-Tube interview between Jeff Goins and Bob Baker on December 5, 2013 in which Goins was asked, "If you could identify one book that changed your life, what would that be and why did it change it?" His answer may no longer surprise you: "I love the book *"The Alchemist* by Paul Coelho." Goins went on to say he reads it regularly and that it has great principles; it shows us not to settle for anything less than fulfilling your dreams.[11] Seth Barnes tells his readers in *Kingdom Journeys* that Goins took his mentoring better than anyone else, and it looks like he did.

Jeff Goins has since authored three other books, become quite the blogger, and is now teaching others how to write. In the interview with Bob Baker he says he feels called to this work—compelled to do this—that perhaps it is *a "nudge from the Muse or a call from God."*[12] To use the term Muse in the same breath as God is another sad indication of the occult leanings Goins has. In Greek mythology, the nine muses were the goddesses "who gave inspiration (breathing in) of the powers of speech and poetry."[13] Goins told Baker that he is also in the process of writing another book about finding your calling—something, he says, that drives us—something "that will bring life to the world."

Michael Hindes is a certified Trainer, Coach and Speaker for The John Maxwell Team (Emergent) and is founder of Kingdom, Inc.[14] He also has his own online coaching website.

****

NOTES

Chapter One: An Open Letter to Ingrid Schlueter, VCY Crosstalk America, Concerning Adventures in Missions (AIM)

1. Seth Barnes. "Responding to unfair criticism." January 8, 2010 <http://www.sethbarnes.com/? filename=responding-to-a-ridiculous-criticism>.
2. Chelsea DiPaolo. "The places that used to fit me cannot hold the things I've learned." <http://michaelhindes.com/post/738732897/the-places-that-used-to-fit-me-cannot-hold-the-things> emphasis added.
3. Seth Barnes. "It's not biblical." January 28, 2008. <http://www.sethbarnes.com/?filename=its-not-biblical>.
4. Seth Barnes. "Mission trips as "spiritual formation." September 6, 2010 <http://www.sethbarnes.com/?filename=stms-as-spiritual-formation>.
5. Seth Barnes. "4 Aids to personal growth." April 3, 2007 <http://www.sethbarnes.com/index.asp?/filename=4-aids-to-personal-growth>.
6. Andrew Shearman. "Becoming god with skin on." June 18, 2008 <http://www.sethbarnes.com/?filename=andrew-shearman-4>. Seth Barnes posted this under his category, 42nd Generation. It includes a video of an interview between Barnes and Shearman.
7. Ronald Miller and The Editors of New Age Journal. *As Above So Below: Paths to Spiritual Renewal in Daily Life* (New York: St. Martin's Press, 1992), p. 96.
8. Seth Barnes. "John Eldredge on community living." June 30, 2007 <http://www.sethbarnes.com/?filename=john-eldredge-describes-the-world-race>.
9. Seth Barnes. *The Art of Listening Prayer* (Gainesville, GA: Praxis Press, Inc., 2005), p. 22.
10. Ibid., p. 23.
11. Ibid., p. 21.
12. Seth Barnes. "Interpreting Scripture – a few things to consider."

84 / *Mission, Mysticism & Magic*

January 29, 2008
<http://www.sethbarnes.com/?filename=interpreting-scripture-a-few-t...>.

13. Seth Barnes. "It's not biblical." January 28, 2008
<http://www.sethbarnes.com/?filename=its-not-biblical>.

14. Seth Barnes. "On being spiritual." August 8, 2006
<http://www.sethbarnes.com/index.asp?filename=on-being-spiritual>.

15. Steven Mitchell. "An Open Letter to Calvary Chapel Pastors of America Concerning YWAM." February, 2002
<http://www.deceptioninthechurch.com/ywamopenleter.html>.

16. Seth Barnes. "Heidi Baker expects miracles – so should you." February 8, 2008 <http://www.sethbarnes.com/?filename=heidi-baker-expects-miracles-so-should-you>.

17. Seth Barnes. "Lakeland revival: A post-Bentley analysis." August 15, 2008
<http://www.sethbarnes.com/?filename=lakeland-revival-a-postmortem-analysis>.

18. "Todd Bentley at Lakeland, Florida!" The Christian Expositor.
<http://www.thechristianexpositor.org/page138.html>.

19. Guy Chevreau. *The Toronto Blessing: An Experience of Renewal and Revival: Catch the Fire.* (1994. Toronto, Canada: HarperPerennial-HarperCollinsPublishers Ltd., 1995), p. 53.

20. Mark & Patti Virkler. *How to Hear God's Voice: An Interactive Learning Experience* (Shippensburg, PA: Destiny Image Publishers, Inc., 2005), p. 21.

21. Ibid., p. 45.

22. You can watch this deceptive episode at <http://www.sidroth.org/site/News2?page=NewsArticle&id=8639&news_iv_ctrl=0&abbr=tv>. Similar episodes can still be viewed such as WSTK-ITV-Sid Roth Interviews Mark Virkler on "Hearing the Voice of God" at <https://www.youtube.com/watch?v=sWxSwuACE08> and "How to Hear God's Voice – Sid Roth Interviews Dr. Mark Virkler" at <https://www.youtube.com/watch?v=WX14uUi8DUw>

23. Michael J. Holden. "Increasing the Anointing." CWG Ministries. June 2001 <http://www.cwgministries.org/Journaling-Example-2.htm>.

24. Barbara Marx Hubbard. *Emergence: The Shift from Ego to*

Essence (Charlottesville, VA: Hampton Roads Publishing Company, Inc., 2001), pp. 40-42.

25. Barbara Marx Hubbard. *The Book of Co-Creation, The Revelation: Our Crisis is a Birth* (Sonoma, CA: The Foundation for Conscious Evolution, 1993), p. 63.

26. Dave Hunt. "New Age Inroads into the Church." July 1, 1989 <http://www.thebereancall.org/print/5919>.

27. Seth Barnes. *The Art of Listening Prayer*, pp. 109-110.

28. Jeff Goins. "The Importance of Leaving Home." October 15, 2007 <http:wwwburnsidewriterscollective.com/social/2007/10/the_importance_of_leaving_home.php>.

29. Jeff Goins. "Adventures in Missions 'World Race' for January 2011." <http://www.christiannewswire.com/news/2838315114.html>.

30. Seth Barnes. "Your false self." August 22, 2009 <http://www.sethbarnes.com/?filename=your-false-self>.

31. Seth Barnes. "Rohr on becoming a spiritual warrior." January 24, 2007 <http://www.sethbarnes.com/index.asp?filename=becoming-a-spiritual-warrior>.

32. Richard Rohr. *Enneagram 11: Advancing Spiritual Discernment* (New York, NY: Crossroad, 1995), back-cover.

33. Matthew Fox. *The Coming of the Cosmic Christ* (San Francisco: Harper & Row Publishers, 1988), p. 79.

34. Ibid., p. 137.

35. Ibid., p. 7

36. Michael Toms, *At the Leading Edge* (Burdett, NY: Larson Pub., 1991), p. 52.

37. "Wisdom School: CAC Conferences." This was an online advertisement from Rohr's Center for Action and Contemplation about an upcoming 5-day Wisdom school conference in New Mexico, May 1-5, 2011 with Richard Rohr and Rev. Cynthia Bourgeault teaching on contemplative prayer, lectio divina, and more, in order to "facilitate the opening of what is classically known as 'the third eye.'" <http://www.cacradicalgrace.org/conferences/2011/wisdom/> emphasis added.

38. Seth Barnes. "Richard Rohr: A Conversation." December 13, 2007. <http://www.sethbarnes.com/?filename=richard-rohr-a-conversation>.

39. Ibid.
40. Seth Barnes. "Your false self." August 22, 2009
    <http://www.sethbarnes.com/?filename=your-false-self>
    emphasis added.
41. Seth Barnes. "Eldredge on our identity in Christ." January 18,
    2008 <http://www.sethbarnes.com/index.asp?filename=we-
    have-all-forgotten-what-we-really-are-and-how-cruci...>. If you
    can't pull up this old web address, try his new one at
    <http://www.sethbarnes.com/?filename=we-have-all-forgotten-
    what-we-really-are-and-how-crucial-our-identity-in-christ-is>.
42. Richard Rohr. *Everything Belongs: The Gift of Contemplative
    Prayer,* rev. & updated ed. (New York, NY: Crossroad
    Publishing Company, 2003), pp. 181-182.
43. Seth Barnes. "Who do you trust your identity to?" May 29, 2008.
    <http://www.sethbarnes.com/?filename=who-do-you-trust-your-
    identity-to>.
44. Ibid.
45. Seen in "The Importance of Leaving Home" by Jeff Goins and
    the Parent's Guide written up by AIM for those going on the
    World Race mission trip.
46. Seth Barnes. It's not biblical." January 28, 2008, and
    "Deliverance ministry – a story of how it works." January 27,
    2008 <http:www.sethbarnes.com/?filename=deliverance-
    ministry-a-story-of-how-it-works>.
47. Seth Barnes. "Vote for Jesus this presidential election." June 26,
    2007 <http://www.sethbarnes.com/?filename=vote-for-jesus>.
48. Seth Barnes. "So what's the big idea?" July 23, 2010
    <http://www.sethbarnes.com/?filename=so-whats-the-big-idea>.
49. Seth Barnes. "How God spoke to me this morning." June 13,
    2009 <http://www.sethbarnes.com/?filename=how-god-spoke-
    this-morning>.
50. Seth Barnes. "The 42nd generation will cross into the promised
    Land (pt. 5)." May 26, 2008
    <http://www.sethbarnes.com/?filename=the-42nd-generation-
    will-cross-into-the-promised-land-pt-5> emphasis added.
51. Seth Barnes. "What is the 42nd Generation?" May 18, 2008
    <http://www.sethbarnes.com/index.asp?filename=what-is-the-
    42nd-generation>.
52. Seth Barnes. "The 42nd generation will change the world (pt. 6)."
    May 27, 2008 <http://www.sethbarnes.com/?filename=the-42nd-

generation-will-change-the-world-pt-6>.
53. Ibid., emphasis added.
54. Seth Barnes. "What is the 42nd Generation?"
55. This is taken from Part 4 of 5 of the Adventures in Missions interview series between Seth Barnes & Andrew Shearman. You can watch Part 4 at <http://vimeo.com/1092250>.
56. Ibid. Andrew Shearman 4
57. Ibid.
58. Ibid. This is also stated in Seth Barnes post, "Andrew Shearman: Becoming God with skin on.: June 18, 2008 <http://www.sethbarnes.com/?filename=andrew-shearman-4> emphasis added.
59. Andrew Shearman 1. Taken from Part 1of the AIM interview series found at <https://vimeo.com/1091834>.
60. Andrew Shearman 2. Taken from Part 2 of the AIM interview series found at <https://vimeo.com/1092092>.
61. Andrew Shearman 3. Taken from Part 3 of the AIM interview series found at <https://vimeo.com/1092196>.
62. Andrew Shearman. 5. Taken from part 5 of the AIM interview series found at <https://vimeo.com/1092512>. You can also look up Seth Barne's posts about the 42nd generation concept on his blog under the category, "42nd Generation."
63. Jeff Goins. "The Day Before a Pilgrimage." September 30, 2009 <http://jeffgoinsmyadventures.org/?filename=the-day-before-a-pilgrimage-with-ten-other-men>.
64. There are numerous sources to retrieve information about Pierre Teilhard de Chardin and his influence within the New Age movement, many of which come from New Age authors themselves. One such source is *Harper's Encyclopedia of Mystical & Paranormal Experience* by Rosemary Ellen Guiley (HarperSanFrancisco, 1991). *Trojan Horse: How the New Age Movement Infiltrates* the church by Samantha Smith & Brenda Scott (Lafayette, LA: Huntington House Publishers, 1993), which I contributed writing and research to, also devotes a few pages to the influence and beliefs of Teilhard de Chardin (pp. 140-143).
65. Jeff Goins. "Mini-pilgrimages." October 3, 2007 <http://jeffgoins.myadventures.org/?filename=minipilgrimages&bookmark=true>.
66. Jeff Goins. "The Importance of Leaving Home." October 15, 2007

<http:wwwburnsidewriterscollective.com/social/2007/10/the_im
portance_of_leaving_home.php>.
67. Jeff Goins. "Mini-Pilgrimages." October 3, 2007
<http://jeffgoins.myadventures.org/?filename=minipilgrimages&
bookmark=true>.
68. Life Positive's "interview with Brazilian spiritual fiction writer,
Paul Coelho" titled, "Sorcery – Everybody is a magus."
<http://www.lifepositive.com/spirit/traditional-
paths/sorcery/coelho.asp>.
69. Paul Coelho. *The Alchemist* (New York, NY: HarperOne-
HarperCollins, 1998), p. 12-13.
70. Ibid., p. 139.
71. Ibid., pp. 152-153.
72. Rosemary Ellen Guiley. *Harper's Encyclopedia of Mystical &
Paranormal Experience* (HarperSanFrancisco, 1991), p. 6.
73. Nevill Drury. *Dictionary of Mysticism and the Esoteric
Traditions* (Garden City Park, NY: Prism-Unity, 1992), p. 9.
74. The Telegraph. "Eternal search for soulmate." May 25, 2008
<http://www.telegraphindia.com/1080525/jsp/calcutta/story_931
5792.jsp>.
75. Paul Coelho. *The Pilgrimage* (New York, NY: HarperOne-
HarperCollins, 1992), back-cover.
76. Ibid., p. 143.
77. Ibid., pp. 230-231.
78. Ibid., pp. 232-233.
79. Ibid., pp. 256-257, emphasis added.
80. Ibid., p. 258.
81. Ibid., p. 260.
82. Jeff Goins. "The Resurgence of Pilgrimage, Pt. 4: Why we need
a pilgrimage." February 22, 2008
<http://jeffgoins.myadventures.org/?filename=the-resurgence-of-
pilgrimage-pt-4-why-we-need-a-pilgrim...>.
83. Comment by a reader named Aart to the post by Jeff Goins,
"The Importance of Leaving Home," emphasis added.
84. Jeff Goins. "Christian Pilgrimage: Homesick at Home." March
2, 2010. <http://jeffgoins.myadventures.org/?filename=christian-
pilgrimage-homesick-at-home>.
85. Seth Barnes. "You can be a hero." October 29, 2009
<http://www.sethbarnes.com/?filename=you-can-be-a-hero>
emphasis added.

86. Jeff Goins. "So Beautiful by Len Sweet and other Free Books." May 4, 2009 <http://jeffgoins.myadventures.org/?filenmae=so-beautiful-by-len-sweet-and-other-free-books>.
87. Leonard Sweet. *Quantum Spirituality* (Dayton, Ohio: Whaleprints, 1991), p. 312.
88. David Spangler. *Reflections on the Christ,* 3ʳᵈ ed. (Scotland: Findhorn Publications, 1981), pp. 40-41.
89. Ibid., p. 45.
90. Seth Barnes. "Spiritual direction: advice from a soul friend." September 14, 2007 <http://www.sethbarnes.com/index.asp?filename=spiritual-direction-advice-from-a-soul-friend>.
91. Seth Barnes includes the link to All Saints Parish: Celtic Spirituality. "Celebrating Eleven Years of Celtic Spirituality at All Saints Parish." <http://allsaintsbrookline.org/celtic.html>.
92. "Feast of Samhain/Celtic New Year/Celebration Of All Celtic Saints." <http://allsaintsbrookline.org/celtic/samhain.html>.
93. Ibid.
94. "Shape-Shifting Mediation." <http://allsaintsbrookline.org/celtic/meditation.html>.
95. Caitlin & John Mathews. *The Encyclopedia of Celtic Wisdom* (1994. Rockport, MA: Element Books Limited, paperback edition, 1996), p. 146.
96. Claris Van Kuiken. *Battle to Destroy Truth: Unveiling a Trail of Deception* (Manassas, VA: REF Publishing, 1996).
97. Brenda Scott & Samantha Smith. *Trojan Horse: How the New Age Movement Infiltrates the Church* (Lafayette, LA: Huntington House Publishers, 1993), Chapter 3: "Jesus Christ: A Druid?"
98. Jeff Goins. "Everyone's a Heretic But Me." August 23, 2009 <http://jeffgoins.myadvenures.org/?filename=everyones-a-heretic-but-me>.
99. Adventures in Missions' "Parents' Guide." (p. 2 when downloaded from website address).
100. Ibid., p. 4
101. Ibid., p. 2.
102. Ibid., pp. 6-7, emphasis added.
103. Ibid., p. 3.
104. Ibid., p. 5, emphasis added.
105. Ibid., p. 6, emphasis added.
106. Ibid., p. 7, emphasis added.

107. "The World Race: About the Missions Trip."
<http://www.theworldrace.org/?tab=about&subtab=training-camps&tuid=4966681>.

108. Ibid.

109. "Parent's Guide," p. 2

110. Seth Barnes. "Another Story of raising the dead."
October 16, 2006 <http://www.sethbarnes.com/?
filename=another-story-of-raising-the-dead>.

111. CBN online, "Spiritual Gifts: 'Intimacy for Miracles.'"
<http://event.cbn.com/spiritualgifts/event/?EventID=11>.
Update: This website, unfortunately, now says, "This event
is now over. Thank you!" You can no longer view the video
at this address. However, there are plenty of other You-
Tube videos you can find with Heidi Baker and other leaders
in the Charismatic/Pentecostal movement displaying and
promoting similar deceptive behavior.

112. Iris Global (previously Iris Ministries). "About Us."
http://www.irisglobal.org/about>.

113. Allen Boehm. "Why won't this dead guy walk?" November
21, 2010
<http://allanboehm.theworldrace.org/?filename=why-wont-
this-dead-g...> emphasis added. Seth Barnes also
reposted this on his blog at
<http://www.sethbarnes.com/?filename=why-wont-this-
dead-guy-walk>.

114. Erika Baldwin. "Life in Him." Posted by teammate, Justine
Zins in Germany, July 15, 2010
<http://justinezins.theworldrace.org/>. Note: In the 1st
Kindle Edition of this book, there was #9: "I used to think
raising the dead only happened the 3 or whatever many
times that it happened in the bible." Although this was also
posted by Justine Zins, it was a quote by another teammate,
Jamie Neumann, from her post, "I Don't Care What I Think
Anymore," dated July 14, 2010.

115. Kathryn Gironimi. "The Silence: Day 2." October 14, 2010.
<http://kathryngironimi.theworldrace.org/?filename=the-
silence-day-2>.

116. Annie Besant. *Esoteric Christianity* (1901. Wheaton, IL: The
Theosophical Publishing House, 1987), pp. 26-27.

117. Seth Barnes. "Is all truth God's truth?" November 12, 2010

<http://www.sethbarnes.com/?filename=is-all-truth-gods-truth>.

118. Seth Barnes. "Everybody follows somebody, who do you follow?" October 17, 2007 <http://www.sethbarnes.com/?filename=everybody-follows-somebody-who-do-you-follow>.

Chapter Two: Mysticism, Miracles & Magic: The Deception Continues

1. Jeff Goins' response to my Open Letter to Ingrid Schlueter posted January 19, 2011 on the Crosstalk Blog.
2. Comment posted by Michael Henry on the Crosstalk Blog, January 19, 2011.
3. Seth Barnes. "The critics and listening prayer." January 25, 2011 <http://www.sethbarnes.com/?filename=the-critics-and-listening-prayer>.
4. Seth Barnes. "Does Jesus still raise the dead?" December 20, 2010 <http://www.sethbarnes.com/?filename=does-jesus->.
5. Seth Barnes. "More dancing, laughter and healing." March 9, 2012 <http://www.sethbarnes.com/>.
6. Michael Hindes. "Provoking Again." March 2, 2011 <http://michaelhindes.com/> .
7. Ibid.
8. Ibid.
9. Ibid.
10. Jeff Goins. "What I'm Reading This Week." March 27, 2011 <http://goinswriter.com/reading-3- 27-11/>.
11. Squidoo Community. "Missionary, Marketer, Writer." <http://www.squidoo.com/jeffgoins>.
12. Ibid.
13. Marion Weinstein. *Positive Magic: Ancient Metaphysical Techniques fro Modern Lives* (Franklin Lakes, NJ: New Page Books, 2002), p. 11, emphasis added.
14. Ibid., p. 15, emphasis added.
15. Ibid., p. 216.
16. Gareth Knight. *Magic and the Western Mind: Ancient Knowledge and the Transformation of Consciousness* (St. Paul, MN: Llewellyn Publications, 1978), pp. 2-3.
17. Ibid., p. 17.
18. Seth Barnes. "What permission do you need?" March 3, 2011

<http://www.sethbarnes.com/?filename=what-permission-do-you-need>. Note: This was posted in the category, Spiritual Formation.
19. Ibid.
20. Helen Schucman. *A Course in Miracles: Text* (Tiburon, CA: Foundation for Inner Peace, 1975), p. 13.
21. Barbara Marx Hubbard. *The Book of Co-Creation, The Revelation: Our Crisis is a Birth* (Sonoma, CA: The Foundation for Conscious Evolution, 1993), pp. 245-246.
22. Ibid., p. 259.
23. Marianne Williamson. Poem: "Our Deepest Fear." <http://skdesigns.com/internet/articles/quotes/williamso n/ourdeepest_fear/>.
24. Helen Schucman. *A Course in Miracles: Manual for Teachers* (Tiburon, CA: Foundation for Inner Peace, 1975), p. 83.
25. Marianne Williamson. *Everyday Grace; Having Hope, Finding Forgiveness, and Making Miracles* (New York, NY: Riverhead Books, 2002), pp. 4-5.
26. Ibid., p. 3.
27. Ibid., p. 12.
28. Megan Thomas. "God in a Box." October 27, 2010 <http://meganthomas.theworldrace.org/?filename=god-in-a-box>.
29. A. J. Wagoner. "'By your powers combined...'" February 16, 2011 <http://ajwagoner.theworldrace.org/?filename=by-your-powers-combined>.
30. Ibid.
31. Robby Riggs. "Provoking Christ in Humanity." May 13, 2011 <http://robbyriggs.theworldrace.org/?tuid=8784070> emphasis added.
32. Marianne Williamson. *Everyday Grace*, p. 257, emphasis added.
33. Ibid., p. 254.
34. Ibid., p. 145.
35. Ibid., p. 145.
36. Mike Nagel. "Is it Worth It?" November 11, 2010 <http://youthworkers.adventures.org/?filename=is-it-worth-it>.

Chapter Three: The Occult Significance Behind 11:11

1. Sara Choe. "A World Race Manifesto?" December 1, 2010 <http://updates.theworldrace.org/?filename=a-world-race-manifesto>.
2. Ibid.
3. Ibid.
4. Rosemary Ellen Guiley. *Harper's Encyclopedia of Mystical & Paranormal Experience* (HarperSanFrancisco, 1991), p. 410.
5. "Numbers meanings numerology—Esoteric significance of numbers." Posted by Aymen Fares on July 26, 2011. <http://www.spiritual.com.au/2011/07/numbers-meanings-numerology...>.
6. Simone M. Matthews. "2009: The Magic of a Universal '11' Year." December 28, 2008. This was posted in her Universal Life Tools & Practitioner directory website at <http://www.universallifetools.com/2008/12/2009-the-magic-of-a-universal-11-year/> emphasis added.
7. Carol Kelley. "2011 - A Year and Season of Great Transition for EVERYONE! HEARING God is Certain!" November 26, 2010 <http://www.elijahlist.com/words/display_word/9361>. This article was also posted on facebook by Heaven Bound, November 27, 2010 at <http://www.facebook.com/note.php?note_id=157518374293367&id=315978873261>.
8. Simone M. Matthews. "11:11 Doorway." 2006 <http://www.universallifetools.com/article_detail.php?recordID=21>.
9. Carol Kelley. "2011 - A Year and Season of Great Transition for EVERYONE! HEARING God is Certain!"
10. Ibid.
11. Synthia Esther. "Numerology Occult Magick – The Power Behind the Force." © 2009-2010 <http://www.sacredpursuit.org/gpage33.html>.
12. Ibid.

Update

1. For more detailed information on Ron Walborn, see http://whputnam00.blogspot.com/2013/09/christian-missionary-allince.html>. The writer of this blog, who I have, gratefully, come to know, has well-documented research on Walborn's teachings and connections.

2. Thomas Merton. *New Seeds of Contemplation* (1961. New York: New Directions Publishing Corp., 1972), pp. 156-157.

3. Ibid. pp. 294-295.

4. <http://www.adventures.org/GlobalAction/cga-bios.asp>.

5. "Center for Global Action: Expectations" <http://www.adventures.org/globalaction/expectations.asp>.

6. "Center for Global Action: FAQs" <http://www.adventures.org/globalaction/faqs.asp>.

7. "Missional Food and Life: Sustainable Agriculture & Living For Missional Communities." <http://missionalfoodandlife.wordpress.com/>.

8. <http://missionalfoodandlife.wordpress.com/aim/>.

9. <http://missionalfoodandlife.wordpress.com/curriculum/>.

10. <http://www.moodyradio.org/chrisfabrylive/>.

11. "016 – Jeff Goins interview, From Zero to Hero in Two years – The Creative Entrepreneur." December 5, 2013 <http://www.diycareermanifesto.com/2013/12/jeff-goins-writer-inerview.html>. Baker's question starts around the 35.08 mark.

12. Ibid.

13. Barbara G. Walker. *The Woman's Dictionary of Symbols & Sacred Objects* (HarperSanFrancisco, 1988), p.76.

14. <http://simplykingdom.org/the-hindes/>.

ABOUT THE AUTHOR

Claris Van Kuiken is author of *Battle To Destroy Truth: Unveiling a Trail of Deception* (1996), her personal account of what took place within a four-year period after she found both subtle and blatant occult teachings were being upheld as Christian in her church and Christian school her daughter attended. She was also the contributing author and researcher for *Trojan Horse: How the New Age Movement Infiltrates the Church* (1993), by Samantha Smith and Brenda Scott. For over 25 years, Mrs. Van Kuiken has been researching and exposing the many ways in which New Age/occult beliefs and practices are penetrating America, its churches and Christian schools—under the guise of being Christian. She's lectured in several states and Canada, and has been a guest on Christian talk radio. As a free-lance writer, Mrs. Van Kuiken has contributed articles to the *Christian Renewal* (Canada) and Illinois Family Institute.

Made in the USA
Columbia, SC
22 March 2018